# ROMANS
# ON THE
# RHINE

# Books by Paul MacKendrick

THE MUTE STONES SPEAK

THE GREEK STONES SPEAK

THE IBERIAN STONES SPEAK

ROMANS ON THE RHINE

# ROMANS ON THE RHINE

## Archaeology in Germany

*Paul* Mac*Kendrick*

**Funk & Wagnalls**

NEW YORK

For Andy, with love

# FOREWORD

This book, like its predecessors, *The Mute Stones Speak* (New York, 1960), *The Greek Stones Speak* (New York, 1962), and *The Iberian Stones Speak* (New York, 1969), is an attempt to write cultural history from archaeological evidence. The evidence has been drawn from an area wider than that indicated by the title. It includes selected sites in the Roman provinces of Belgica, Raetia, Noricum, and Pannonia, as well as the two Germanies, Upper and Lower; in modern terms, parts of Holland, Switzerland, Austria, and Hungary as well as West Germany. (The Romans gave up any attempt to penetrate the area of what is now East Germany after the disaster of A.D. 9.) I particularly enjoyed, as I hope the reader will, the field trip along the Limes which resulted in Chapter Four, "The Wide Frontier."

The dedication expresses inadequate thanks to my son, who drove expertly on that pleasant occasion. I owe particular thanks also to Professor Hans Schönberger and his efficient staff at the incomparable library of the Romisch-Germanische Kommission in Frankfurt-am-Main where most of my research was done; to Dr. Hans Kulmbach of the Romisch-Germanisches Zentralmuseum in Mainz; and to the authorities in Augst, Avenches, Bern, Bonn, Copenhagen, Köln, Mainz (Mittelrheinisches Landesmuseum), Munich (Landesamt für Denkmalpflege), and several others indicated under Acknowledgments at the back of the book, who supplied photographs in a true scholarly spirit. The Rheinisches Landesmuseum in Trier sold me permission to reproduce pictures.

I again express hereby thanks to my colleagues E. L.

*Foreword*

Bennett, Jr., and J. P. Heironimus for their meticulous proofreading. Professor Heironimus has also earned the reader's gratitude, and mine, for his painstakingly accurate translation of the passage on Caesar's bridge (pp. 28–29).

—P.L.M.

*Madison, Wisconsin*
*December, 1969*

# CONTENTS

# Contents

# ILLUSTRATIONS

# Illustrations

**xiv**

# Illustrations

# ROMANS
# ON THE
# RHINE

# 1 : *Before the Romans*

HEN the Romans first came into the Rhine valley, they did not find the land unoccupied. What were they like, these Germans the Romans failed to conquer? An ancient German has obligingly returned from the grave to tell us (Fig. 1.1). During World War II, Danes digging peat in Jutland to alleviate the coal shortage hit upon a body, miraculously preserved in the Tollund bog. His high forehead and aquiline nose give him an aristocratic appearance, but his diet was plebeian and his end ignominious. Analysis of his stomach contents showed that he had been eating only vegetables and grain, and his cervical vertebrae had been broken, probably by hanging. Other finds, bodies, skeletons, and skulls, show that the early Germans were a mixed lot, far from a master race, with an average height of only five feet six.

We should not be surprised at evidence of early Germans coming from Denmark. The original home of the Germanic tribes—who were not a single, unified people, and who never called themselves Germans—was roughly within a 300-mile radius of present-day Copenhagen. Seeking living space (*Lebensraum*), they exerted pressure on the peoples to the south and southwest—the Celts—whom they drove across the Pyrenees into Spain and across the Alps into Italy. Thus the sack of Rome in 390 B.C. by "the Gauls" was due ultimately to German pressure behind them.

The Romans first met the Germans—the tribes of Cimbri and Teutoni—in 113 B.C., and the meeting was not cordial. In the next eleven years the Germans defeated five Roman

3

1.1 Tollund man

consular armies—on at least one occasion hanging the
Roman generals from convenient trees—and it took the
military genius of the Roman commander Marius to beat
them at Aquae Sextiae (Aix-en-Provence) in 102, and at
Vercellae (Vercelli) in north Italy in 101 B.C. The victories
were for the moment decisive: the soil of Aix was fertilized
with the blood of 100,000 Germans; its vineyards were
fenced with bleached German bones. But forever after the
Romans feared the *furor Teutonicus*, and the confrontation
brought home to Rome the need, for her own security, to
control the lands beyond the Alps.

The next Roman general to face the Germans was

Marius' nephew Julius Caesar, who saw in defeating them a chance to build his own prestige. To enhance the story of his ultimate victory, he told how reports of the Germans' enormous stature, piercing eyes, unbelievable courage, and incredible military skill had at first shattered the morale of his officers and men. But he annihilated them in 58 B.C. near Mulhouse in the plain of Alsace (see map, Fig. 1.2), and only a miserable remnant, including the German chief Ariovistus, escaped across the Rhine. An anti-Caesarian senatorial investigating committee in Rome was to find Caesar guilty of atrocities, and recommend that he be handed over to the enemy. Caesar ignored the recommendation.

To stop German interference in Gaul, Caesar built his famous bridge across the Rhine—to be described in more detail in the next chapter—but withdrew after eighteen days, destroying his bridge behind him. It was his practice in his *Commentaries* to hide his reverses behind digressions, and it is his digression on the Germans that interests us here. It is second-hand and inaccurate, his aim being to propagandize, not to record sober anthropological fact. His Germans turn out to be more-or-less noble savages, dividing their time between warfare and stock-rearing, possessing no private property. They are milk-drinkers and meat-eaters —both practices bizarre to wine-drinking and pasta-eating Italians: eating meat gave Romans diarrhoea. The Germans are mighty hunters, undisciplined, but they keep their huge bodies in the pink of condition. They go in for mixed bathing in icy rivers, and dress in skins. Their economics are primitive. What they chiefly want is an export market for the spoils of war. Their horses are small but well-trained; they ride bareback. They have reduced to a no-man's land the territory for ninety miles along their frontier. They worship the sun, moon, and fire, are remarkable for their chastity, and deliberately deny themselves worldly goods in order to keep themselves from becoming domesticated, greedy, spoiled, and discontented. They submit to government only

in time of war. They support themselves by raids upon their neighbors, but regard hospitality to the stranger as a sacred duty. They are more primitive than the Gauls, and dwell in an endless forest populated by fabulous animals like the unicorn, the aurochs, and the elk. (Since Caesar on the elk is the only joke he permits himself in his entire works, it is perhaps worth recording here. Elks have no knee-joints, and so must sleep leaning against trees. According to Caesar, the canny Germans, knowing this, saw trees partway through, wait for the wretched animals to lean and fall, and then move in at leisure to perform the happy dispatch.)

Germany has had distinguished early historians: not only Caesar, but Cornelius Tacitus, who published a twenty-five-page essay on the Germans in A.D. 98, when the Romans had been in contact with them for 210 years. "That is the time it is taking," says Tacitus, "to conquer Germany." The essay's full title in one manuscript is *On the Origin, Geography, Customs and Peoples of the Germans*, and this adequately covers the contents. Tacitus depends on secondary sources, and, being of a turn of mind both moralistic and gloomy, loses no opportunity either to compare German noble savagery with Roman decadence or to condemn Germans for vices like sloth, a universal lust for gambling, or beer-drinking. Archaeology sometimes confirms, sometimes contradicts his statements; for example, dice are found in only the richest German graves.

The first half of his *Germania* is general, the second particular. Tacitus begins with geography and climate, which isolate the Germans, for, as he remarks with Italian prejudice, "Who would leave Asia, Africa, or Italy to visit Germany, with its unlovely scenery, its bitter climate, its general dreariness to sense and eye, unless it were his home?" Some

**1.2 Map: German and Celtic sites**

have been unkind enough to infer that this remark implies personal experience. No one could write about Germany with this venom, it is alleged, unless he had actually lived there. Certainly the sons of Italy, serving in the legions in Germany, found the climate and the people equally fierce.

Tacitus peddles the myth of German purity of race—blue eyed, strawberry-blond—which, as we have seen, archaeology disproves. He describes Germany as a forest wilderness, which it was not, though it was more heavily wooded than it is today. On the other hand, archaeology confirms his statement that German cattle were undersized. For rhetorical effect, he claims that Germans despise gold and silver, a point disproved by finds of precious metal in German graves. Archaeology strikingly confirms, by the absence of coins, that the Germans of the interior had, as Tacitus says, a barter economy.

To project his image of the Germans as noble savages, Tacitus alleges that they use very little iron. Archaeology bears him out in part: little chain-mail, few swords or metal helmets, but plenty of shields and lances.

Turning to religion, our author states that the Germans practice human sacrifice, have no temples, and never represent their gods in human form. These statements archaeology partly confirms and partly denies. A famous silver cauldron (Fig. 1.7)—Celtic, not German—found dismantled in a peat bog at Gundestrup in Denmark, does indeed portray human sacrifice, but a number of German temples and statues of gods have been found. There is, however, also evidence for open-air sanctuaries, confirming Tacitus: "They do not deem it consistent with the divine majesty to imprison their gods within walls . . . Their holy places are the woods and groves, and they call by the name of god that hidden presence which is seen only by the eye of reverence." Tacitus describes the Germans casting lots before embarking on an enterprise: just such lots have been found in a prince's grave at Dorotheenhof in West Prussia. A sacred wagon such as he mentions was found in a bog in Jutland (Fig. 1.3).

1.3 Dejbjerg, cult wagon

Tacitus states that the Germans are not city-dwellers, but live scattered, "where spring, plain, or grove has taken their fancy." This remark is borne out by the hundreds of modern German place names ending in -brunn, -feld, and -wald. But German villages have been excavated, and they are not unplanned. One, at Feddersen-Wierde, just north of Bremerhaven, had detached houses, as Tacitus says, but they were arranged radially around a central open space, approached by streets or alleys with wickerwork footways. The settlement, in which seven habitation levels have been distinguished, is raised on an artificial mound, which served instead of a dike to protect it from the incursions of the North Sea. The houses are long and narrow, with animal stalls attached, so that man and beast lived under one roof. The stalls are arranged either side of a central walkway, laid with wickerwork to keep the farmers' feet out of the manure. In early phases a hedge surrounds several houses; later, each house has its own hedge. The archaeological reading of this is that an early clan structure broke down with time. Feddersen-Wierde also illustrates the strong social differentiation stressed by Tacitus. One house, dated by pottery and *fibulae* (the ancient safety pins: see Fig. 3.17) in the second or third century A.D., is distinguished from the others by being hedged and ditched, by the number of barns adjoining, and by the concentration near it of

**9**

metalworkers' shops. At Fochteloo in Holland an impressive chief's house adjoins a humble village (Fig. 1.4).

Tacitus writes about the punishment of cowards, shirkers, and perverts by drowning them in swamps and holding them down with frames of wickerwork. Exactly such burials have been found in the bogs of Schleswig-Holstein. The

1.4 Fochteloo, manor house

woman whose body was found in Borremose, Denmark, buried with the switches she was whipped with, her head partly shaved, was probably taken in adultery.

The moors have yielded remains of clothing that bear out Tacitus' account. These remains include a beautifully woven blue plaid from Thorsberg, pieced furs of different colors, and plenty of trousers—to a Roman, a sure sign of barbarity. Tacitus says the Germans often fastened their cloaks with a thorn instead of a *fibula,* and in fact surprisingly few *fibulae* have been found in German graves.

Writing of German food and drink, Tacitus shows an Italian scorn for beer, "a drink corrupted," he says, "into a certain similitude to wine." Traces in the bottom of excavated bronze vessels and drinking horns have proved on analysis to be of fermented barley and berries, or of honey, which would make mead. Since these vessels come mostly from women's graves, it would appear that brewing was done by the distaff side.

In keeping with his noble-savage theme, Tacitus will have it that the Germans change their plowlands yearly, plant no orchards, fence off no meadows, water no gardens. The archaeological evidence is that their fields were long in use, and fenced, and that they knew and used mineral fertilizers.

Tacitus' statement that the Germans burn a man's arms and armor, and sometimes his horse, upon his funeral pyre is contradicted by the excavated graves, where remains of weapons or bones of horses are extremely rare.

In the second half of his essay Tacitus treats the Germans tribe by tribe. The Batavians, ancestors of the Dutch, who had revolted in A.D. 69, were by Tacitus' time pro-Roman, though not Romanized. Tacitus has high praise for the military ability of the Chatti (modern Hessians), who held out against the Romans until well into the reign of Domitian (A.D. 81-96), an Emperor whom our author particularly despised. On the other hand, to the Cherusci, who lived in the Harz mountains, and whose king was financed by Domitian, Tacitus is very unfair, calling them slovenly and slack.

In general, the historian's striving for rhetorical point leads him to praise most highly the most anti-Roman German tribes. For example, the Chauci, who lived on both banks of the Weser, had been on the Roman side in the fatal battle of the Teutoburg Forest (A.D. 9), but later turned to brigandage, and fought the Romans in the Batavian revolt. Tacitus calls them one of the noblest peoples in Germany, righteous in their dealings, unvexed by greed or lawless ambition, living in unaggressive but well-

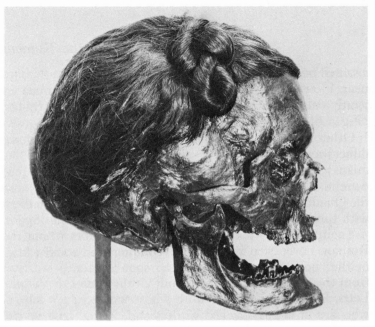

1.5 Österby, hair style

armed seclusion. But Pliny the Elder, who had been Roman procurator in Belgica and knew Germany at first-hand, describes the Chauci as a primitive and poverty-stricken fisherfolk. Pliny is likely to be nearer right.

When Tacitus comes to the Cimbri, he digresses to treat the long and painful history of over two centuries of Roman reverses at German hands, reverses so severe, and so glossed over, that the Germans "have in recent times supplied us with more triumphs than victories"—a dig at the hated Caligula and Domitian, who dyed the hair of Gauls and marched them in trumped-up triumphal processions.

About the Suebi, who under their chief Ariovistus made so much trouble for Julius Caesar, Tacitus tells us only of their distinctive hair style, of which an example from Osterby is on display in the Schleswig Museum (Fig. 1.5).

The Langobardi, from the lower Elbe, who were to wreak so much havoc in Italy long after Tacitus' time, are to him noteworthy for their religious observances, which involved a sacred boat, perhaps like the much later one from Nydam near Flensburg (*ca.* A.D. 350), seagoing, clinker-built of sturdy oak, with thirty-six oars and a capacity of forty-five (Fig. 1.6).

Other tribes mentioned by Tacitus who were to make difficulties for the Romans were the Marcomanni (Bohemians), who fought the philosopher-Emperor Marcus Aurelius successfully for fifteen years (A.D. 166-180), and the Quadi, from the Carpathian Mountains, who were to go with the Vandals to found the Swabian kingdom in Spain.

Tacitus devotes his last four chapters to tribes whom the Romans never even attempted to conquer, and about whom neither he nor they knew much: soot-blackened warriors from the Sudetenland and Poland; Goths from the Vistula; Letts, Lithuanians, Esthonians, whose women are warriors, who live at the ice-packed world's end, in the land of the midnight sun, and thrive on the amber trade. He ends with tales of fabulous creatures, half-man, half-beast (sea cows?) who lived among the ancestors of the Hungarians, Finns, and Laplanders.

South Germany before the Romans had a different history, and it is primarily archaeology that tells it: Baden-Württemberg and Bavaria have no Caesar or Tacitus to

**1.6 Nydam, boat**

1.7a Gundestrup cauldron

recount their story. What archaeology reveals here is a Celtic culture, not entirely driven out by the German invaders. It survives in the place names: Württemberg, for example, comes from the same Celtic root as Verdun. The Celts, as Caesar remarks in passing, were more civilized than the Germans. One piece of evidence for this is their richly ornamented art. A striking example is the silver cauldron from Gundestrup, now in Copenhagen, already mentioned as portraying human sacrifice (Fig. 1.7a). Measuring sixteen inches high, twenty-eight inches wide, and weighing twenty pounds, it is ornamented both inside and out. On the outside are four gods and three goddesses. One god grips in his fists a pair of sea horses; another holds a brace of stags by the hind legs; a third, little men; the fourth is flanked by free figures: a horse curvets on his shoulder. Of the goddesses, one is flanked by birds, another by children. The third has a tiny dancer on her shoulder, and, beside her, Hercules fighting the Nemean lion.

Five panels decorate the inside. There is a goddess with two griffins and a wolf; above her are two elephants. On a second panel (Fig. 1.7b) sits cross-legged an antlered god.

14

1.7b  Gundestrup cauldron, panel

We know his name: he is Cernunnos, dispenser of benefits, emblem of strength and fertility, guardian of the lower world. In one hand he holds the torque, the Gallic neck-ring of twisted metal; in the other a ram-headed snake. Flanking him are a stag, bulls, lions, dogs or wolves, and a man riding a dolphin. The god in the third panel holds a wheel, which a man wearing a helmet embellished with bull's horns is trying to turn. Surrounding the central figure are winged griffins, a horned serpent, and dogs or wolves. The fourth panel portrays the purification of an army off on a campaign. A giant figure plunges the human sacrifice head-downward into a cauldron. The sacrifice is to Teutates (the Roman god Mercury), to the Celts the god of mountain tops and springs, who watched over roads and commerce, and had power over the world below. The troops being purified are pictured in two registers. Above, four horsemen, wearing helmets with totemic symbols (horns, wheel, bird, boars) ride off following a horned serpent. They wear spurs, which were unknown in this part of the world before the first century B.C.: this dates the cauldron. Below are six infantrymen with oblong Celtic shields, followed by a chief, sword on shoulder, and three musicians pointing straight into the air huge trumpets with dragon mouths. The final panel portrays three men with drawn swords pointed at three bulls. Dogs run ahead, leopards bound above. In the bottom of the cauldron is a bull, with the man who killed or sacrificed it, and his dog.

This work of art is obviously not merely a piece of rich decoration. It also reflects a complex mentality. Without literary sources, we do not know enough about Celtic religion to explain it fully, but enough of the motifs appear in the art of other cultures to make it clear that the Celts in Germany, before the Romans came, did not live in cultural isolation. The antlered god and the human sacrifice are pure Celtic. The sea horses and griffins are east Greek, Hercules is a part of Greek mythology, the elephants, lions, and leopards are Asiatic. Experts date the cauldron in the first century B.C., and say it is east Celtic, from somewhere on the upper reaches of the Danube. How it got to faraway Denmark is a puzzle. What is clear is that the artist who made it was at least dimly aware of Greek artistic and religious conventions, which came to him up the river from the Black Sea.

Also on the Danube, above its steep west bank about thirty miles southwest of Ulm, looms on a man-made height a Celtic fortress. From its top is visible on a clear day the Zugspitz in the Bavarian Alps. This is the Heuneburg, the richest and most interesting archaeological area in south Germany. Like the Gundestrup cauldron, it shows Greek influence, but of a much earlier date. It was first dug in 1876, when Schliemann was excavating the gold-rich grave-circles of Mycenae, but the most important discoveries have been made since 1948. One of its excavators, Kurt Bittel, has won fame for his work at the Hittite citadel of Boghaz-Köy, in Asia Minor. Since the war it has been used as a "teaching dig." Trainees have come from England, France, Italy, Yugoslavia, Austria, Sweden, Spain, and Czechoslovakia, learning to read the earth in trenches like that at Urmitz, shown in Figure 1.8.

**1.8 Urmitz archaeological strata**

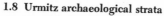

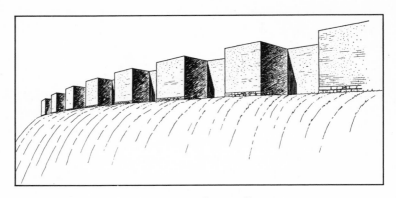

1.9 Heuneburg wall

What makes the Heuneburg important is an imposing 400-foot stretch of wall, belonging to its second-oldest level, on the northwest side (Fig. 1.9). It has eight projecting bastions, each twenty-five feet square, at ten-meter intervals. The wall is ten feet thick and thirteen feet high, built four-square and plumb of plastered sundried brick on stone footings, imitating the expert technique of the walls of Greek Gela in Sicily or Old Smyrna in Asia Minor.* Fragments of Attic black-figure vases, from the late sixth century, help to date the wall, and establish the Greek influence upon it. A gold spoon found near one of the bastions hints at its vanished wealth. One can imagine a Celtic prince, his ancestors buried a quarter of a mile away in the Gresübel mound, which yielded finds hardly less rich than Schliemann's: a ceremonial wagon and harness, gold, bronze, weapons, amber, and Greek pottery. Rich from the profit of amber and slaves, the prince marries a well-dowered Greek girl from Marseilles—Massiliote pottery was found on the site—and imports a Greek-trained foreman and masons to build her a castle, whose imposing façade and imported technique symbolize his princely power and cos-

* See *The Greek Stones Speak*, Figure 3.8-9.

mopolitan connections. By the fourth century the Heuneburg lay in ruins, destroyed in all probability by the Germanic invaders.

The period 800-500 B.C. to which the Heuneburg belongs
is called Hallstatt, after an iron-mining center in Austria,
near Salzburg, where in 1846 was discovered the largest
prehistoric cemetery then known. Its finds are matched in
richness only by those of Mycenae, Etruria, and Scythia.
A nineteen-year campaign explored nearly 1,000 graves and
catalogued over 6,000 objects: pins, brooches, girdles, neck-
laces, earrings, all with geometric and animal motifs; iron
daggers, spear points, axes; bronze cauldrons, fine pottery,
and gold work. Another 1,500 graves have been dug since,
and 500 more still await the spade.

The next Celtic phase—from 500 B.C. to the Christian
era—is called La Tène, after a site on the north shore of
Lake Neuchâtel where typical artifacts were found in 1857.
La Tène art is highly stylized and abstract, full of vegetable
motifs—palmettes and vine tendrils—and volutes; and of
fantastic monsters and demons. Classical control is missing:
the art is dynamic. One rich La Tène site is Kleinaspergle,
north of Stuttgart, where in 1879 a huge unrifled burial
mound yielded a rich store of Etruscan bronzes (a basin a
yard across, and a handsome pitcher decorated with grin-
ning monsters on lip and handle), two gold drinking horns,*
their points decorated with Scythian ram's heads, a silver
necklace, a gold brooch set with coral (Fig. 1.10). The
excavator's seventeen-year-old son, fascinated by the richness of it all, returned one evening to the mound, and discovered by lantern light two Greek vases, which had been
lovingly repaired in antiquity with bronze and gold rivets.
These he carefully packed in his knapsack, and proudly
took home to his father. Not only were they interesting in

---

* The drinking horn, so often found on German sites, confirms Tacitus'
remarks about German intemperance. The point about a drinking horn is
that you cannot set it down, but must drink its contents to the dregs.

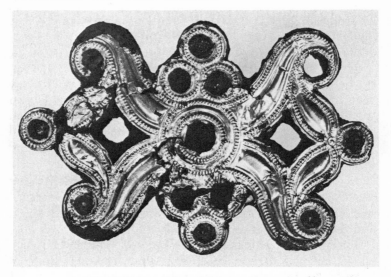

**1.10 Gold brooch from Kleinaspergle treasure**

themselves, but they dated the burial, for one of them, a red-figured cup portraying a priestess at an altar, was identified as the work of the Amymone painter, who was working in Athens between 460 and 430 B.C.

Another La Tène site is Reinheim, east of Saarbrücken, where in 1952 workers in a gravel pit hit upon a Celtic grave. It was not until two years later that the richest treasure—now on display in the Saarbrücken museum—was found: the grave of a Celtic princess, which yielded a gold torque, bracelets and rings; a bronze mirror with a coral-inlaid Janus-head handle; two iron brooches overlaid with gold leaf; a bronze *fibula* in the shape of a cock, with feathers carefully rendered, and coral inlay; a unique ring of glass and tin; and another of bronze; an amber amulet in the shape of a human foot; beads in amber, jasper, and quartzite, and in glass paste in rainbow colors; a fine iron chain dating from a time when iron was still a rare or precious metal; a chalcedony spear point; a quartzite pendant, and another in bronze in the shape of a human figure; a gold rivet, and a scrap of white linen with a purple stripe.

The princess was not only richly bejeweled, but also supplied with an elegant bronze service for eating and drinking in the next world: bronze plates with wooden covers; pierced gold rims of drinking cups in *repoussée*; and the prize of the collection, a slim, elegant gilt bronze pitcher (Fig. 1.11) with a lid surmounted by a horse with a bearded human head; on the handle a bearded man and a ram's head; the body divided into zones delicately incised with lotus blossoms. Parallels to this piece are known from far-away Luristan in Persia; the rings are Etruscan; the animal motifs are Scythian or Thracian. This nameless princess without a castle was rich and cosmopolitan; this land that was one day to blossom with Roman villas was not inhabited by savages before the Romans came.

**1.11  Bronze pitcher from Reinheim treasure**

At Manching, five miles southeast of Ingolstadt on the Danube, is another important Celtic site, discovered in the process of building a military airfield in 1936. What was hit upon was a whole Celtic city, capital of the tribe of the Vindelici: streets, houses, workman's quarter, the whole surrounded by a wall whose perimeter—four-and-a-half miles —is nearly as great as Republican Rome's, and much larger than such Roman cities in Germany as Köln or Trier. The area enclosed is nearly 1,000 acres. The excavators found that not all of it was built over; part of it was a place of refuge for men and cattle in time of raids. With German meticulousness, they counted the animal bones they found. The total was 276,428, mostly of domesticated animals: 2,500 pigs, 1,600 stunted cattle, 1,550 sheep and goats, 250 dogs, 189 horses, and 30 roosters.

The air-photograph, compared with the plan (Fig. 1.12-13), shows the enormous extent of the walled area, and also how the field boundaries respected the line of the fortification, which was obviously part of a master plan expressing a sovereign will. The modern outer fort of Ingolstadt is within the area of Celtic Manching; the Munich-Nürnberg Autobahn passes just to the west, following the line of the prehistoric amber route: the Celts built Manching deliberately at the point where this crossed the main east-west road along the Danube. Half a mile of the wall was destroyed to build the 1936 airfield; further stretches were dismantled for antiaircraft batteries in World War II, or blown up by Allied bombing. There are still thirteen-foot-high stretches of the wall preserved, but it is much ruined. A local motorcycle club was barely prevented from building a racetrack on top of it. Road-building, plowing, and stone-robbing have taken their toll, and building the airfield took priority over systematic excavation.

One of the first finds in 1936 was a hoard of Celtic silver coins; in 1955 was found a silver service—Roman, not Celtic —which proves that Manching was still inhabited after the

Roman occupation. In 1955 airport repairs made possible the digging—with a bulldozer!—of Leisenhartfeld in the middle of the walled area. It yielded tools, pottery, iron spear points, swords and bucklers, bracelets and beads, probably made locally, of colored glass—yellow, red, blue, green, and polychrome—and part of a harness in bronze, decorated with the head of a bird and an ox. Experts dated it in the period called La Tène D, about 100 B.C. As often, local possessiveness interfered with scientific archaeology. A farmer who found a heap of bronze pins refused to give them up because his children were using them for playthings.

The model in Munich of a section of the Manching wall (Fig. 1.14) shows its earlier and later phases. The stretch in the foreground is typical Celtic construction, in which a heavy wooden scaffolding is filled with rubble and faced with smoothly worked stones. In the later phase (background), the face of the wall was extended outward a little more than two feet, and upright posts were driven in to heighten it by means of a palisade. An earthwork nearly forty feet wide slopes inward from the back of the wall; streams were diverted to supply the moat in front. The construction consumed over 100,000 cubic yards of stone, whole forests of wood, and tons of nails.

Within the wall, bulldozed trenches about thirty inches wide struck evidence of a settlement stretching for about a half a mile each way from the center. The houses were of wood, long and narrow, as at Feddersen-Wierde, and oriented north and south. One hundred and sixty wood-lined storage pits for grain prove that the Manching Celts produced a surplus. The Celts knew about crop rotation and fertilizing, and invented the wheeled plow and a mowing machine.

They were experts at metallurgy: the excavators found jet nozzles for copper smelting under forced draft. There was a smithy within the walls, equipped with all the neces-

1.12 Manching, air view

1.13 Manching, plan

**1.14 Manching, stretch of wall, model**

sary tools: files, chisels, punches, tools for engraving and chasing metal, hammers, and tongs. The finds of hinges and keys imply a bourgeois standard of living and values; imported surgical instruments imply the presence of that blessing of civilization, the physician. Molds for making coins show that this important Celtic city had its own mint. The local die-makers altered their Greek models, whether from incompetence or from a desire for abstraction is a vexed question. Most of a hoard of gold coins found in nearby Irsching in 1858 was sold (Prince Albert bought a dozen); part of the profit went to build a new schoolhouse. Manching produced wheel-made pottery: the only imports found were the large pointed amphoras in which oil and wine were shipped from Italy.

Just on the edge of the Autobahn, a mile southwest of

Manching's wall, is a rectangular area surrounded by a ditch. Such sites—some 250 are known—used to be taken for forts, but now the view is that they are Celtic sanctuaries. The largest, the Goloring near Koblenz, is not a rectangle but a circle 568 feet in diameter, walled and ditched, with an approach 130-feet wide, and a mound in the middle with a cavity for a Maypole. Its excavator has compared the Goloring, in design and function, with Stonehenge. We can imagine the wild dancing, the bold riding, that accompanied the rites of passage celebrated there or at Manching.

Civilized as it was, with its developed crafts and industry, its money economy, Manching tempted Roman greed. In a destruction level dated about 15 B.C., the excavators found the bones of eighty-one human beings. Over half of them were under forty. These were Celtic warriors, annihilated by the future Emperor Tiberius in the name of Romanization. As Tacitus makes a Scottish chief say of this aspect of Roman imperialism, "They make a desert, and they call it peace." This is typical Tacitean exaggeration, or half-truth. Manching lies in what was afterward the Roman province of Raetia, with flourishing cities (to be described later) like Augusta Vindelicum (Augsburg), Cambodunum (Kempten), and Regina (Regensburg). The anchor-point of the frontier—the Raetian Limes—was to be fixed only fifteen miles to the northwest. Behind that frontier, the Celts and the Germans who survived and behaved were to enjoy the blessings of the Roman peace.

# 2 : A Bridge and
# Three Colonies

C<small>AESAR</small>'s bridge across the Rhine near Andernach (see map, p. 60) built in ten days in the summer
of 55 B.C., marks Rome's first (and impermanent) penetration into Germany. Caesar specifically states that his pur-
pose in crossing the Rhine was simply to make a demonstra-
tion, in order to punish past and discourage future German
aggression, and to make a gesture of support to the pro-
Roman Ubii.

Caesar's description of his bridge is complicated, its
interpretation controversial. There is a model (Fig. 2.1) in
the Andernach museum, based on Caesar's Latin text, and
on remains of a similar bridge (Fig. 2.2) in the river Waal
at Zuilichem, in Holland. Here is what Caesar says, refer-
ring to himself in the third person, as usual:

*He adopted the following plan for the bridge. He took
logs, a foot and a half in thickness and sharpened a little
distance from the end, and fastened them together in pairs
[number 1]. Their length was proportional to the varying
depth of the river. He lowered them into the water by der-
ricks and drove them in with pile-drivers, not perpendicu-
larly as piles are usually driven, but leaning forward so that
they sloped downstream. Then he set another pair of logs
[2], similarly joined, forty feet downstream, this pair facing
upstream. A beam two feet in width [3] (the distance between the logs of each pair) was let in from above into this*

space, and the two pairs were thus braced against each other with two brackets at each end of the beam [4]. When the pairs were thus held apart and constrained toward each other, the structure was so firm and its parts so devised that the stronger the force of the current, the more tightly it held together. The trestles thus formed were covered by timbers [6] laid at right angles to them, and then by long poles and wickerwork [7]. Moreover, on the downstream side, piles were driven at a more pronounced slope [8]. These, when connected with the whole structure, were to act like buttresses against the current; other piles [5] were also driven in on the upstream side, separated from the bridge by a small space, so that if the barbarians sent down tree trunks or boats to dislodge the structure, the shock of such assaults might be lessened by these buffers and the bridge escape injury.*

There were also buffers or fenders on the upstream side (not shown in the model), to break the force of the impact in case the natives tried to demolish the bridge by floating down tree trunks or beams. The model differs from others in its interpretation of the words "the two pairs were thus braced against each other," which are taken, on the evidence of the remains of the Zuilichem bridge, to imply not a truss construction, as in a barn roof, but the addition of a third pile at a more oblique angle. According to the model-builders, Caesar's description is hard to understand because he is attempting an account, not of the whole bridge, but only of the innovations introduced by his engineers.

Caesar crossed his bridge, received delegations, demanded hostages from tribes requesting peace and friendship, and destroyed the villages, farm buildings, and crops of the hostile Sugambri. Having achieved, as he says, the object of his crossing, he prudently refrained from accepting the

* Tr. by J. P. Heironimus.

29

2.1 Andernach, Caesar's bridge, model

challenge of the main enemy, the Suebi, and, as we saw, retired across the Rhine into Gaul, destroying his bridge behind him. He had been in Germany exactly eighteen days.

Two years later he built another bridge, probably at Neuwied, a little above where he had crossed before, and made another sortie into Germany, to punish the Germans for reinforcing the Gauls, and to prevent their giving asylum to a refugee Gallic chief, Ambiorix. This time the Suebi retreated into their forest fastness, and Caesar, fearing overextended supply lines, again prudently refrained from pursuit. However, so as not to let the natives think they had seen the last of him—though in fact they had—he broke down only the German end of his bridge, and heavily fortified and manned the Gallic end.

Whether from scorn or from respect, Caesar had nothing further to do with the Germans. Toward the Swiss, his attitude was firmer. He planned two colonies in the area (see map, p. 6o): Colonia Julia Equestris (Nyon, on Lake

**30**

**2.2 Zuilichem, Roman bridge, remains of piles**

Geneva), and what was later called Colonia Augusta
Raurica (Augst, near Basel). The Swiss had helped the
Gallic resistance-leader Vercingetorix, and were not to be
trusted. The founding of Nyon (Fig. 2.3) is dated by a
coin in either 50 or 49 B.C. It has a colonnaded forum (II
on the plan), Roman drains, mosaics (one with a Cupid
aquaplaning on an amphora), an aqueduct, temples and
shrines: a typical small provincial replica of Rome itself.

At Augst, excavation began as long ago as 1582. Renaissance humanist archaeologists knew, as all archaeologists
must, their history: one must dig in books as well as in the
earth to make the mute stones speak. They knew that the
founder of the Roman colony at Augst was L. Munatius
Plancus, a friend and legate of Julius Caesar, and appointed
by him the first governor of Transalpine Gaul. Plancus'
tombstone, still in place at Gaeta in Italy, on the coast
above Naples, records that he triumphed over the Raetians
—the Latin name for the Alpine tribes of east Switzerland,
the Tyrol, and Bavaria—and planted colonies at Lyon and
Augst. A Roman triumph presupposes atrocities. Possible
evidence for what Plancus did to earn his emerged in 1942

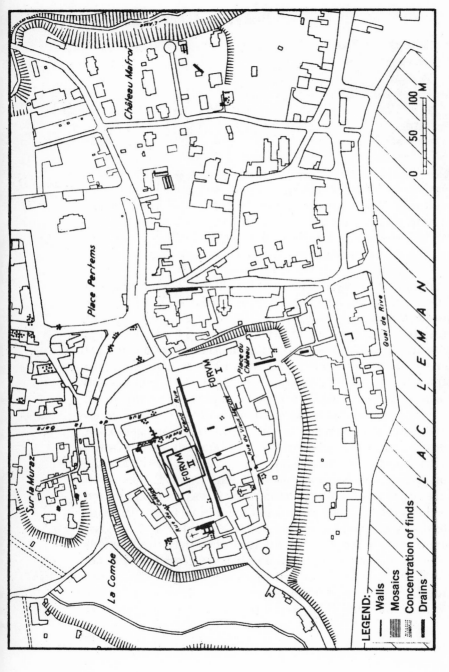

2.3 Nyon, plan

LEGEND:
Walls
Mosaics
Concentration of finds
Drains

LAC LEMAN

0   50   100 M

Château Mafroi

Place Pertems

Sur la Muraz

La Combe

FORVM I

FORVM II

Place du Château

Rue du Vieux Marché

Quai de Rive

just north of Basel: a mass grave, in which most of the bodies were children.

We know that Plancus was in his province in 44 B.C., and in Rome for his triumph in 43. The street plan of Colonia Raurica has been found to be oriented on the midsummer sunrise, June 21, 44 B.C., just over three months after the man who had appointed Plancus was assassinated. The veterans who got houses and land at Augst could be trusted to react like 100-percent Romans if any of the surviving natives showed themselves ungrateful for the manifold blessings of the Roman peace. What two of the survivors looked like is revealed in two striking bronze heads (Figs. 2.4 & 2.5) now in the Bern Historical Museum.

The site of Augst was chosen because it commanded communications: between Italy and Germany, and between Gaul and the Danube valley. The location seemed ideal to the ancient city planner: on high, defensible ground between two brooks feeding into the Rhine a half-mile away. The spot where the surveyors set up their measuring rod on that midsummer day in 44 B.C. became the sacred focal point of the colony. A line drawn due north and south through this focal point runs directly through the city gate on the south and the Rhine fort of Kaiseraugst on the north.

Since the excavators have found nothing Roman that is datable before 15 B.C., their assumption is that for its first thirty years the colony was simply a military installation, with wooden barracks. Only when Augustus, after a personal inspection tour, concluded that the area was secure did Augst begin to take on the aspect of a carefully and handsomely planned civilian settlement. The planners must have felt safe, for excavation shows that until the Alemanni threatened in A.D. 233 Augst had no protective walls. At the surveyor's focal point (plan, Fig. 2.6, XI) rose the altar and

2.4 Prilly, bronze bust of man

2.5 Thun-Allmendingen, bronze bust of woman

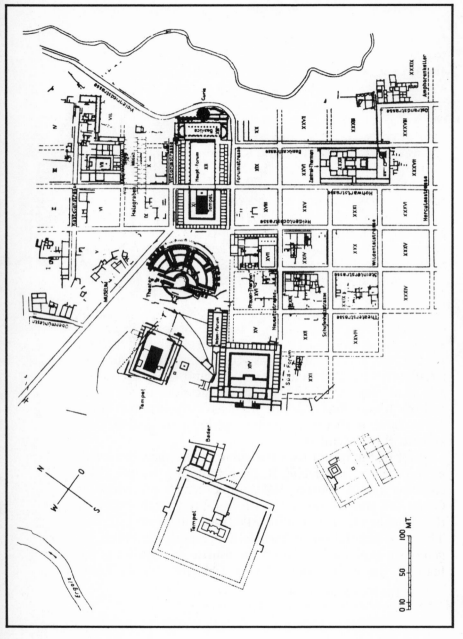

2.6 Augst, plan

temple of Jupiter, its precinct surrounded with shops. An inscription dates it in A.D. 145, but this was a remodeling: the excavators found traces of an earlier, simpler phase. Facing it was the porticoed main forum (XII), also girt with shops, and paved with red sandstone. At the east end of the forum, facing the temple, was the basilica, for law courts and market. Within, columns divided it into a nave and two side aisles. Its north and south ends, in this phase, curved into apses, as in Trajan's basilica in Rome * (A.D. 113), but the masonry technique at Augst was not in use till a generation later. Through the center of its east wall, on an axis with the altar of the Jupiter temple, the ninety-eight town fathers used to enter their round curia, or council house (see model, Fig. 2.7), with the town treasury in its basement. The masonry style of the curia shows that it was a later addition to the basilica, built in the early third century A.D.

Between forum and temple ran the colony's main north-south street, the Decumanus Maximus. At intervals of 180 feet on either side of it ran five parallel streets. North and south of the forum-temple axis—the line of the Cardo—ten parallel streets, 215 feet apart, ran east and west to form the grid plan. The proportions between the sides of an Augst city block were thus 6:5. The streets average fifty feet wide. Many have porticoes to protect pedestrians against sun, and—in this climate—rain.

West of the forum rises the curve of the sheer gray wall of the theater, and facing it, on a hilltop, a temple. This combination of theater and temple has a precedent at Ostia, the port of Rome.† Both buildings are oriented in the same direction, and differently from the forum-complex. The new orientation of theater and temple has been ingeniously explained as based on sunrise on April 19, the feast of the grain-goddess Ceres. On this day in Rome

* See *The Mute Stones Speak*, p. 265; paperback, p. 261.
† See *The Mute Stones Speak*, p. 256; paperback, p. 254.

**2.7 Augst, Forum, model**

plays were given in her honor: to her, then, the theater and temple in Augst may have been dedicated.

The theater passed through three phases, all visible in the air-photograph, (Fig. 2.8). The semicircular rows of seats belong to the earliest, perhaps Augustan, phase. About A.D. 73-74 Augst harbored troops, who preferred beast-fights and gladiatorial shows to the more refined pleasures of the stage. For them, the theater was remodeled into an amphitheater, a quarter the size of the Coliseum in Rome. The elliptical outline of its walls runs just above the center and through the lower right quadrant of the photograph. When the troops were withdrawn, perhaps in Hadrian's reign (A.D. 117-138), the stage returned to favor. But this did not mean that the colonists lost their taste for blood sports. In 1959 another amphitheater, without stone seats, was found in a wood about a quarter of a mile southwest of the theater (see plan). Coins discovered in it show that its use began about the time the theater-amphitheater was given up, and continued into the fourth century. Meanwhile, the plan of the theater-amphitheater was altered, so that plays could once more be produced in it. To this third phase, and second theater, belongs the imposing retaining wall in the upper left half of the photograph, and the semicircular orchestra in the center. The retaining wall was not visible in antiquity; its function was to separate the upper and lower sections, and to support the second theater's red sandstone seats, since robbed to supply building materials for the Middle Ages. A break in the center of the back wall of the stage building allowed spectators a view of the temple. Behind the last row of seats ran a portico supported

**2.8 Augst, theater, air photograph**

by columns stuccoed a dazzling white. When the theater was full, the white of the columns, the red of the stonework, and the multicolored dress of the seven or eight thousand spectators must have made a colorful spectacle.

At the time the first theater was in use, the height to the west was not monumentalized. Excavation revealed, in this earlier, simpler phase, an irregular precinct containing a number of modest square buildings, the typical shape, as we shall see in Chapter 6, of what are called "Gallo-Roman" temples. These were for native use, while the Roman colonists worshiped in the pre-Antonine version of the Jupiter temple on the forum. Coins help to fix the date of this first Gallo-Roman phase: 368 of them were found, ranging in time from the Roman Republic through Domitian (who reigned from A.D. 81 to 96), plus one of Antoninus Pius, dated about 150. This, then, will be the approximate date of the second, monumental phase of the temple area. It matches in time the final phase of the theater, and of the Jupiter temple on the forum: it appears that in the middle years of the second century A.D., described by Gibbon as "the period in the history of the world during which the condition of the human race was most happy and prosperous," Augst shared in the prosperity, and monumentalized its public buildings, secular and religious. The new hilltop temple was enclosed within a new triple precinct wall, foursquare and formal. The precinct area had to be built up artificially to make it level; it was supported by three superimposed levels of vaults containing shops and storerooms. A flight of monumental steps provided access to it from the theater.

Prosperity apparently rendered the old forum inadequate, for about A.D. 225—on the stylistic evidence of a bronze statuette of Fortuna (Lady Luck)—a supplementary forum was built southwest of the theater. It is visible in the upper left of the model (Fig. 2.7). One entered at the northeast corner, through a long, narrow pedestrian mall flanked with shops. The new forum proper was a peristyle, with shops on three sides. They are now open-fronted, but slots in the sills show how they could be closed with wooden panels. In the far northwest corner a room with three niches must have been a shrine. It was here that the statuette of Fortuna—a deity appropriate to a commercial area—was found.

Augst was not without its amenities: it had three sets of public baths. In one (plan, XVII), so many hairpins and necklace beads were found that it must have been for women only. Like other buildings of the town, it went through two phases. The first, which resembles in plan the Stabian Baths at Pompeii, should be dated, like them, in the 70s A.D.: it was better adapted to a southern than to a northern climate. Both phases provided the usual sequence of hot, tepid, and cold baths, with radiant heating in floors and walls, that in the floors being actually too hot for bare feet: bathers had to use wooden clogs. But in the second phase, to be dated in the palmy days of the second century A.D., an outdoor pool was abandoned, and even the corridors and the cold-bath room were heated. The plans for the first phase were no doubt drawn up by theoreticians in Rome; the revisions in the second phase reflect practical local experience of inclement northern weather.

The central baths (plan, XXXII and XXXVII) were among the largest in Roman Switzerland. They cover parts of three city blocks, and cut off two streets. To make room for them, houses of the 70s A.D. were cleared away; their cellars underlie the present structure. These baths, enlarged in the second century, are more symmetrical than the women's. They had frescoed walls, a mosaic floor, and a portico facing the afternoon sun. An aqueduct served the baths from the south. For convenience in repairs and cleaning, its vaults were built as high as a man. The channels were lined with waterproof cement (*opus signinum*). Water was distributed from the main in pipes of wood or lead. There was also ample provision of drains, without which no

Roman city planner would have dreamed of building a city.

The baths already mentioned simply kept the colonists clean. Another set, in the Grienmatt area, west of the new forum, restored their health. These have special bathtubs, and adjoin a temple precinct where thank-offerings to Aesculapius, god of health, were found. No doubt this sanatorium attracted not local clients merely, but pilgrims from a wider area. A building south of the main grid, with a large yard for horses and wagons, multiple heated rooms, and baths, was probably an inn for the use of these and commercial travelers. Another more elegant hostelry in the northern quarter (plan, VIII) was for important personnages. The pilgrims' gratitude for cures is expressed in the richness of the building in the center of the precinct. This was two-storied, long and narrow, with two richly decorated façades, and semicircular statue-niches. Its nearest parallel is the ornamental façade called the Septizonium, built in Rome in A.D. 203 at the southeast corner of the Palatine Hill, facing the Via Appia, and greeting visitors from the south with a symbol of the grandiosity, and questionable taste, of the Severan dynasty.

Southeast of the Grienmatt sanatorium, on the high ground between the new forum and the amphitheater, another Gallo-Roman temple was discovered by accident. It turned up in a photograph (Fig. 2.9) taken by Swissair in the extraordinarily dry summer of 1950. The temple was in use in the early Empire, and formed an architectural counterpoint to the classical temple behind the theater. The remains of yet another Gallo-Roman temple, its cella, a principal room, curiously sunken below the level of its colonnade, were destroyed when a new highway was put through in 1963.

The rest of the fifty blocks of the town was given over to private houses. The excavation of some of these inspired the building of a unique adjunct to the site museum: the Römerhaus, a Roman provincial dwelling reconstructed

2.9 Augst, Sichelen temple before excavation, air view

with elements copied from all over the Roman world: window-frames after originals from a refuse heap at Vindonissa, a window-grill and a mosaic from a villa at nearby Hölstein, and numberless details from Pompeii and Herculaneum. This vivid presentation of how provincial Romans lived, plus the intrinsic interest of the Roman town itself, makes Augst one of the most worthwhile sites to visit north of the Alps.

In general, the simpler houses, with a minimum of frescoes, mosaics, and central heating, belonged to the working class, and contained shops. The most interesting of these were smokehouses, for the preparation of the delicious hams, bacon, and sausages for which the district had long been famous, as we know from a treatise on farming by the Roman scholar Varro, published in 36 B.C. Another shop combined fulling (dry-cleaning), as inferred from a fuller's vat found in it, with weaving: the evidence for the latter is loom weights. There were several bronze foundries. One house, which yielded nearly 500 pounds of scrap metal, must have belonged to a junk dealer. Some of the scraps were fragments of large bronze statues, collected after the barbarian invasion of A.D. 260. They prove that Augst in its

**43**

prime must have contained an impressive number of public monuments. Another house must have been a public bar. It had a fresco of two men carrying a wine jar slung on a pole between them; there were forty more three-dimensional wine jars in the cellar. From House XXX (see plan) came thousands of animal bones, indicating a menu with a gourmet range not often matched in modern Switzerland: suckling pig, kid, hare, goose, chicken, quail, pheasant, squab, snipe, thrush, frogs' legs, and snails. Since such a variety is beyond modest private means, the excavator ingeniously suggests that the building was the clubhouse of a guild.

Northeast and northwest, outside the town, in accordance with the regular Roman custom, were the cemeteries; some gravestones from them are built into the Römerhaus wall. In the eastern cemetery, 1,358 graves have been excavated. Many were Christian: one bears an anchor, symbol of Christian hope, used instead of the cross by those in fear of reprisals, in the bad old days before Constantine's Edict of Toleration in A.D. 313.

To Constantine's predecessor Diocletian is due the fortress of Kaiseraugst, directly on the Rhine, built in haste about A.D. 300 against the barbarian invasion: into its walls are built doorsills, window ledges, column drums and capitals, lengths of architrave (stone beams), inscriptions, and sculpture. The most remarkable find from Kaiseraugst turned up in 1961-1962 inside the wall. It is a treasure of silver; seventy pieces (thirty-six of them spoons, of which replicas can be bought in the Römerhaus), plus medallions, and mint-fresh coins. One of the finest pieces is the eight-sided Achilles plate (Fig. 2.10), stamped with its weight (fifteen pounds), and bearing scenes from the early life of the hero. Starting at "five o'clock," and proceeding counter-clockwise, we see him born; dipped in the river Styx (to make him invulnerable, all but his heel); handed over to the centaur Chiron—half man, half horse—for tutoring;

2.10 Augst, treasure: Achilles plate, silver

nurtured by wild beasts; learning to hunt, to read (a particularly charming scene), and to play the lyre; restored to his mother; disguised as a girl, to save him from the Trojan War; and among the women. The central medallion shows the penetration of his disguise by the wily Odysseus and Diomedes.

The coins can be dated. The latest is of A.D. 350. Since they are mint-fresh, they must have been hidden almost as soon as they were made. They were found, carefully packed in straw, in a chest. They may have been part of the royal baggage of the future Emperor Julian, who was in the area at the time. But the barbarian came down like the wolf on

**45**

the fold; the royal owner never recovered his property, which had to wait over sixteen centuries to see the light of day. Riches threatened by barbarian hordes: this is the story of the decline and fall of the Western Empire everywhere. There is a certain appropriate irony in the fact that Augst, which rose and flourished with the Empire, should also decline and fall with it. But what matters most is the archaeological evidence for the long years of prosperity, which, without the Romans, the little city would never have had; indeed, without the Romans, it might never have existed.

Six years after Augst was founded to keep the Swiss quiet, Octavian-Augustus' lieutenant Agrippa settled the friendly German tribe of the Ubii on the west bank of the Rhine. This was the beginning of Köln, now the fourth largest city in Germany, after Berlin, Hamburg, and Munich. Roman surveyors "centuriated" the area; that is, they laid it out in lots, their orientation different from that of the later Roman colony. This orientation is marked by the modern road leading southwest to Luxemburg, and by others parallel to it. A camp for two legions (I and XX) covered 150 acres in the northwest quarter of the later colony. At the naval station at Bayenthal, to the south, were berthed ships like the small, fast *liburna* (cutter) shown in the model (Fig. 2.11). While the naval station remained, the camp lasted only until about A.D. 35, when Legion I was moved to Bonn, and XX to Neuss, while the civil authority of the province remained where it was. Hence the history of Köln is of a civilian, not a military center.

Agrippa's granddaughter Agrippina, born in Köln in A.D. 15, grew up to marry the Emperor Claudius. In A.D. 50 she persuaded her husband to elevate her birthplace to the rank of colony, and to settle veterans there. This act makes Köln

officially the oldest city in Germany. Like Augst, it was laid
out on a grid plan (Fig. 2.12); unlike Augst, it had a wall
from the beginning. (The burials at A on the plan, inside
the colony wall, date from pre-colonial days.)

Enough of the triple north gate (plan, H) of this wall
was preserved to make possible the construction of a model

**2.11 Basel, ship model (*liburna*)**

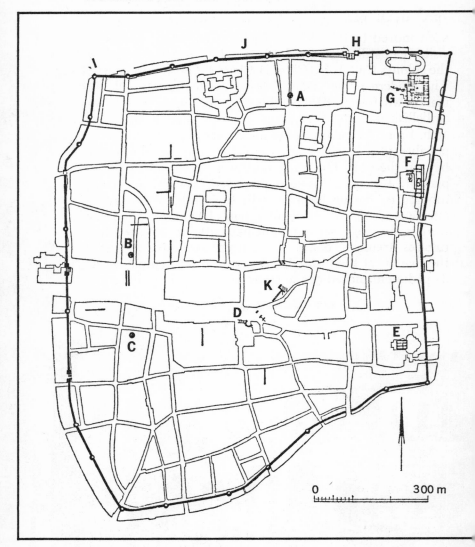

2.12 Köln, plan

(Fig. 2.13), here seen from within. Part of the gate has been moved to the Wallraf-Richartz Museum, where the visitor can still see, carved on its outer face, the initials of the colony: C.C.A.A. (Colonia Claudia Ara Agrippinensis). The modern name "Köln" derives from the Latin "Colonia." Two towers flanked the triple entrance, which was embellished with Corinthian pilasters, like a triumphal arch. From the gallery above, defenders could fire down on possible foes in the court below, or out on the enemy beyond the wall. The wall's northwest tower (Römerturm, plan, I; Fig. 2.14) is also preserved, saved from stone-robbing by having been used in the Middle Ages as the latrine of a convent. At about a man's height, its gray stonework is, uniquely, set in mosaic-like patterns: rosettes, half-rosettes, triangles, bands of lozenge-shaped stones. Just in the shadow at the top right, the pattern is a temple-façade, its pediment picked out in stone of other colors: limestone

2.13  **Köln, north gate, model**

2.14 Köln, Römerturm

and red sandstone. Altogether, Köln's wall had thirty-one
towers and eight gates. It enclosed an area one-fifth the size
of Rome. The workmanship was good: the sturdy northeast
tower had to be dynamited in the nineteenth century to
make room for the footings of the Hohenzollern Bridge
near the Dom. Part of the wall may have been built when
the Ubii were settled on the site, before the Claudian
colony, for some of the finds of pottery are of Augustan
date.

No Roman colony in the West considered itself complete
without an amphitheater and a theater. Köln's amphitheater must have been built partly of wood, for it was
erected in the thinly inhabited area, in a hollow, outside
the north wall (plan, J), to reduce the danger of fire spreading. Two dedications to Diana, goddess of hunting, supply
evidence for its use. One refers to fencing its wild-animal
enclosure, the other evokes the wild frontier: the dedicator
gives thanks that in six months he has caught fifty bears—
obviously for use in the beast-fights. The theater—unexca-

**50**

## A Bridge and Three Colonies

vated—must have faced the forum, in the area between the modern Opera House and the north-south throughway (plan, K). To the southeast of the forum the church of St. Maria im Kapitol (plan, E) preserves in its name and in its foundations the evidence for a three-cella temple, a Capitolium, dedicated to Jupiter, king of the gods; his wife, Juno; and his daughter, Minerva. A colony was incomplete without the dedication of such a temple. The excavators report that this one is to be dated close to Köln's foundation-date of A.D. 50.

Colonial amenities regularly included public baths, as we saw at Augst. But the baths of Köln, southwest of the theater (plan, D) are oriented not on the colonial grid but along the lines of the pre-colonial centuriation. They must have been in existence from the time Agrippa settled the Ubii on the site; i.e., in 38 B.C. or shortly after. Their water supply came from the foothills six miles away to the southwest. Later, in the second century, to meet increasing demand, the aqueduct was extended another forty miles to the mountains of the Eifel. In frost-free Italy, Gaul, and Spain, aqueducts could be carried on handsome lofty arches, but the Köln aqueduct had to be buried, below the frost line. In laying out a green belt in 1927-1928, the workmen came upon a settling-basin of the Köln aqueduct, which is visible opposite Barenratherstrasse 465 at the Beethoven Park. Konrad Adenauer, then Köln's mayor, took an interest in its preservation. Thirty feet below the modern street level, under the restaurant Im Römer, in the Budengasse, between the Dom and the Rathaus, are the vaults (Fig. 2.15), eight feet high, of a water run-off channel that drains into the Rhine. It is built, without mortar, of the volcanic stone called tufa, so honestly put together that it served in World War II as an air-raid shelter.

Köln suffered heavy damage in the war, but at least the bombing revealed Roman ruins. Some of the most interesting of these are under the new Rathaus or city hall, where

**51**

2.15  Köln, vaulted drain

2.16  Köln, Praetorium-Regia, model

one can have the experience of visiting antiquity by elevator. These are the remains (plan, F) of the Roman governor's palace, the earliest phase of which goes back to the founding of the colony. Here the gluttonous Vitellius, the Rhine legions' short-lived candidate to succeed Nero in A.D. 69, was acclaimed Emperor. (He lasted less than a year.) Fire destroyed the banqueting room; Vitellius' comment on the evil omen was, "Courage, men! Light is given us!"

The palace was rebuilt twice after the fire. The model (Fig. 2.16) shows its fourth and final phase, dated by coins to about A.D. 310, in the reign of Constantine the Great. With its impressive arcaded façade overlooking the water, and its octagonal central structure, it closely resembles the palace of Constantine's predecessor Diocletian at Split on the Dalmatian coast. From the colony's east gate, just south of the palace, a bridge ran across to the fortress of Divitia (Fig. 2.17), nowadays Deutz, with its fourteen massive round towers, built under Constantine at the same time as the last phase of the palace. Its sixteen barracks would hold 900 men, an outpost against the Franks.

In its early years, too, the colony had need of its fortifications. In the winter of A.D. 69-70, when Köln was less than twenty years old, the Batavians at the mouth of the Rhine revolted from Rome, and dreamed of an independent Empire. The loyal Ubii, near neighbors of the colonists, were made to suffer heavily for their loyalty. The conspirators met in Köln, and, with the connivance of German troops in the Roman army, plotted the murder of the Roman general Vocula. The German prophetess Veleda, who lived haughtily apart in a high tower, foretold success for the rebels. But the non-German veterans who had colonized Köln, and the German settlers as well, refused to heed rebel advice to tear down their walls, murder the Romans, confiscate Roman property, and abjure Roman decadence. The most they would do was to reduce customs duties, and allow transit through the town, in daylight only, to unarmed

2.17 Köln-Deutz, bridgehead fort, model

travelers. The competent generals appointed by the new Emperor, Vespasian, put down the revolt in A.D. 70, and Köln returned to the even tenor of her ways. The future Emperor Trajan, lovingly known as Optimus Princeps, the best of princes, was serving as governor of Germany, with headquarters in the palace, when he received word of his accession in A.D. 98.

Thenceforward for 150 years the evidence for Köln's history is entirely archaeological, and the tale it tells is one of prosperity. Inscriptions show men from Köln all over the Empire: a procurator in Lusitania, a corporation of merchants in Budapest, a pious dedicator to Jupiter on the Great St. Bernard Pass. And men from all over the Empire —from Spain, from Gaul, from Rome itself—came to live in Köln. What attracted them was the flourishing industry, especially in pottery (kilns, plan B, C) and glass. (The handsome local glassware will be discussed and illustrated in Chapter 7.) The gravestone of a perfumer of the second century A.D. contains what may be the earliest recorded mention of eau de Cologne.

The most impressive evidence for Köln's prosperity during the middle years of the Roman Empire appeared in 1941, when excavation for an air-raid shelter just south of the Dom (plan, G) turned up the House of the Dionysus Mosaic. This is a luxurious residence built round a courtyard with a fountain. It had a long veranda overlooking the Rhine. The mosaic was laid in the two-story dining room in the middle of the east side.

It is divided into twenty-seven medallions, treating three themes: the Dionysus myth, the seasons, and the menu. The central medallion (Fig. 2.18) portrays the wine-god drunk, leaning on a satyr. Other related scenes show satyrs and maenads (the wine-inspired women who worshiped Dionysus) dancing, or playing the flute, lyre, Pan-pipes, castanets, or tambourine. One charming domestic scene shows a satyr family (satyrs were not normally noted for their domesticity). The mother plays the double flute, the father dangles an enormous bunch of grapes above the head of his baby son. A satyr rides a donkey, Cupid rides a lion. Pan leads a billy goat; there is a delightful female leopard with a broad blue ribbon around her neck. Two panels of the seasons survive: in one, representing summer, a pair of parrots draws a cart laden with garden tools; another pair of birds, with a cart full of grapes, symbolizes autumn. Representation of the menu served in the dining room includes oysters, peacock, ducks, cherries, grapes, and pears. At the top, household pets—dogs and a tortoise—are waiting for scraps from the table. The material side of life clearly outweighed the spiritual in the mind of the prosperous proprietor who commissioned this mosaic. From the location of the house on the river it is a reasonable guess that he was a wholesale merchant, perhaps a grain dealer. The mosaic came from pattern-books current about A.D. 220.

Archaeology also testifies to agricultural prosperity. At Müngersdorf, three miles from the colony's west gate, meticulous investigation—involving over 250 trenches, and

2.18 Köln, Dionysus mosaic, detail

**2.19 Köln-Müngersdorf, farm buildings, model**

published in 1933—unearthed a ten-acre walled farmstead whose working life, attested to by pottery and coins, extended from the foundation of the colony until the late fourth or fifth century. The main house (Fig. 2.19), which had twenty-nine rooms (only one of them heated) had weatherproofed walls and a tile roof. It follows the plan of most working farmhouses north of the Alps: tower-flanked verandas, looking west on an orchard, east on the farmyard; and a two-storied courtyard, roofed against the weather. North of the court were the baths, veneered in part in Belgian marble, and provided with a latrine that flushed; south of it were the living quarters. The excavators report the pathetic discovery of the bones of a dachshund and the house cat. The principal room once had a mosaic floor; part of its painted walls survives. The surface was polished with pumice before painting, and waxed after. The colors are loud: a Pompeian red field with a green border; the dado stippled brown and yellow. Among the ingredients identified in the colors are iron oxide, ocher, and imported lapis lazuli. The motifs are the conventional ones of what archaeologists call the Pompeian Fourth Style, in vogue there between A.D. 62 and 79: candelabra, grotesques, birds, crossed horns of plenty, sea monsters, plants. In the farmyard were sleeping quarters for the farm hands, and various other buildings identified by dimensions or contents. They include a pigsty, a sheepfold, a stable, and a cow barn (containing milk pails and a cooling-cellar). The owner, who, the excavator thinks, was probably German, and his family

57

were buried on the property: the evidence is six expensive sarcophagi, which prove how rich this family grew. Not one single post-Roman sherd was found, but no trace of burning, either. The inference is that here at least there was no continuity into the Middle Ages. The last occupants simply abandoned the farm, taking their household goods with them.

Less than half-a-mile west of the Müngersdorf farmstead, workmen digging a cellar in 1843 at Weiden hit upon an underground, vaulted grave-chamber whose expensive materials and contents give further evidence of Köln's prosperity, this time in the second century A.D., to judge by the style of the sculpture found in the tomb. The stone door was counterweighted to move up and down like a portcullis. A sarcophagus in the tomb is too wide for the door: it must have been let down through the roof. The tomb interior had twenty-nine niches for ash-urns. In addition, rectangular recesses on three sides were lined with yellow marble carved to represent dining couches, where the dead might be imagined to take a meal with the living, a lugubrious idea that the Romans inherited from the Etruscans. To add to the illusion, each major recess contains an Italian marble bust of its occupant: husband, wife, and daughter; and there are two limestone chairs, carved to imitate wickerwork, each of which when found had an ash-urn sitting on it. There were rich small finds in glass, silver, amber, tortoise shell, bone, ivory, and chalcedony. The Etrusco-Roman cult, and the imported Italian marble, lead to the conclusion that the occupants of this tomb were not prosperous German yeoman, like the owners of the Müngersdorf farmstead, but large landowners from Italy.

Their being here, and prospering, had its first cause in Caesar's building his bridge across the Rhine, but the security they enjoyed had been won by Roman military operations, to be described, from the archaeological record, in the next chapter.

**58**

# 3 : Imperialism, Disaster, Retrenchment (15 B.C.–A.D. 73)

In pursuing the history of Augst and Köln, as archaeology reveals it, we have been carried far beyond the dates of their founding, 44 B.C. for Augst, 38 for Köln. It is time now to return to the reign (27 B.C.-A.D. 14) and policy of Augustus, and to induce the mute excavated stones of towns and camps, in Austria, Holland, Germany, and Switzerland, to tell us how his policy of expansion beyond the Rhine was changed by the disaster of the Teutoburg Forest into a policy of retrenchment, followed also by his successors, down to the reign of Vespasian (A.D. 69-79).

Augustus' agent for the intended conquest of Germany was the best general he could find, his stepson Drusus. Drusus fortified the Rhine to provide bases for expeditions eastward, toward the Weser and Elbe. He is said to have built fifty *castella*, several of which (see map, Fig. 3.1) proved of permanent strategic importance, and will be discussed in this chapter. They are Vetera (Xanten), Moguntiacum (Mainz), Vindonissa (Windisch), Bonna (Bonn), and Novaesium (Neuss). In all of them pottery has been

**59**

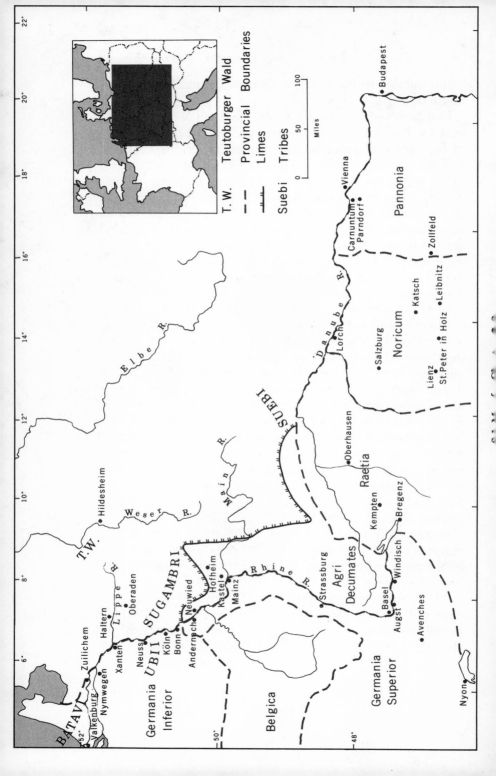

found datable to the years of Drusus' German campaigns, 12-9 B.C.

Drusus based his campaign of 11 B.C. on Vetera, on the west bank of the Rhine opposite the mouth of the Lippe. In the rugged German terrain, armies, as Drusus knew, do well to use water routes whenever possible. Now, some thirty miles up the Lippe, at Haltern, children playing seventy years ago found Roman sherds. These attracted archaeologists, and the resulting excavations revealed a military complex of Augustan date (Fig. 3.2), including what may well have been Drusus' camp. This was an irregular rectangle of a turf wall, protected by a double ditch, enclosing an area of eighty-six acres, large enough for two legions. The potato crop hindered excavation, but trial trenches revealed that within was a later camp, half the size, with an earthwork wall stiffened with wood. Along its main east-west street, the *Via Principalis*, were the remains of wooden buildings: the armory; the praetorium or headquarters building, with the commandant's quarters behind; workrooms, with a sick bay opposite; and barracks. The plan was ingeniously worked out by observing the discoloration of the earth left by postholes. In one of the barracks was found a stock of over 1,000 catapult-arrows, a unique model with a very short shaft. Experiment showed that these would not fire accurately, which may have been why they were left in store: the troops rejected them, as troops in the field since have rejected innovative weapons. This camp showed signs of destruction by burning, perhaps after the Teutoburg disaster laid Roman installations open to German vengeance. A hoard of coins, including one rare gold one, represents the savings of an officer, who never returned to recover them.

The camps were set back from the river. On the bank, workmen digging the cellar of a house found millions of kernels of burnt grain, the stock of a warehouse that had also felt the weight of German retaliation. It had ship sheds,

**61**

and was protected by a wall. It would have served to shield the north end of Drusus' bridge across the Lippe.

Downstream, southwest of the two camps, on a hill called the Annaberg, were found the remains of a palisade and ditch, enclosing a pear-shaped area of seventeen acres, with towers 100 Roman feet apart. This fort would accommodate, in a pinch, half a legion. The finds from it are dated late Augustan. This comparatively small detachment may represent the straits to which the Roman army was reduced after the destruction of Varus' three legions in A.D. 9.

The Haltern excavations have been the casualty of two world wars. In the first, the work was suspended; in the second, the finds were looted. Consequently, it is not now possible to check the results, and the association with Drusus must remain conjectural, not certain. But twenty-five miles upriver, at Oberaden, another camp, three times the size of the second camp at Haltern, provides less equivocal evidence. It contains pottery with the same stamps as those in other Drusus camps, and none of its coins is later than 8 B.C. After that date it was destroyed by fire, and never rebuilt. Apparently Drusus' campaigns were not uniformly successful. But he was not directly responsible for the destruction of Oberaden, for he died in 9 B.C., at the age of twenty-nine, of a fall from his horse. Younger contemporaries associated him chiefly with Germany: it was he who appeared in a dream to the Elder Pliny and inspired him to write his lost history of Germany, on which Tacitus drew. Drusus' death was a landmark to Livy: with it he ended his immensely long 140-book history. And indeed it was the end of a chapter. For Drusus' brother Tiberius, who succeeded him in the German command, was called away in 7 B.C. to put down a major revolt in Pannonia (nowadays Hungary), and operations in Germany marked time, while the Germans consolidated their strength. Drusus was buried in Augustus' mausoleum, and commemorated by the still surviving Arco San Sebastiano, on the Via Appia near the Catacombs in Rome. He had

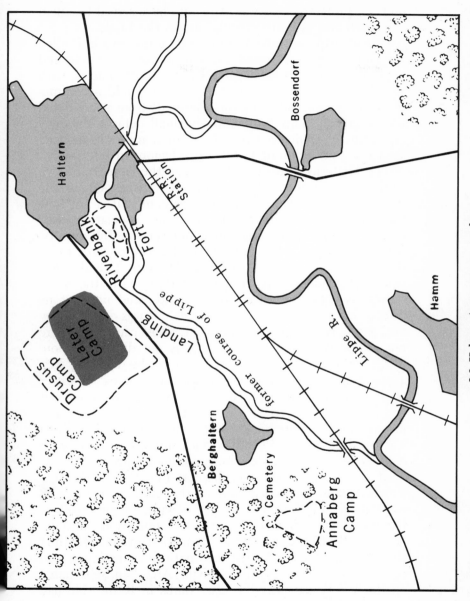

3.2 Haltern, Augustan camps, plan

also a cenotaph—the Eigelstein—in Mainz, and this may be his most significant memorial, for his successes in Germany, like his cenotaph, were empty.

Drusus, however empty in accomplishments, was energetic in action. The earliest levels of the camp at Vetera (also called Xanten, see map, Fig. 3.1) are his: the base, as we saw, for his campaign of 11 B.C. It was of the same shape and construction as his camp at Oberaden, but the details are overlaid by later construction, and cannot be recovered.

In the reign of Claudius (A.D. 41-54), stone buildings at Vetera began to replace wood. The earliest stone building is a *valetudinarium* or sick bay (Fig. 3.3). The well-lighted two-story room behind the entrance was the operating room: in it were found surgical instruments and pharmaceutical herbs. The wards were arranged pleasantly around the courtyard.

The Neronian phase, Vetera I (A.D. 54-68), covered 150 acres, the same as Oberaden. In the central, headquarters building (see plan, Fig. 3.4) the double rooms on three sides of the courtyard held the armory: one room was found full of arrowheads. On the north side of the court was the

3.3 Xanten (Vetera) Claudian sick bay

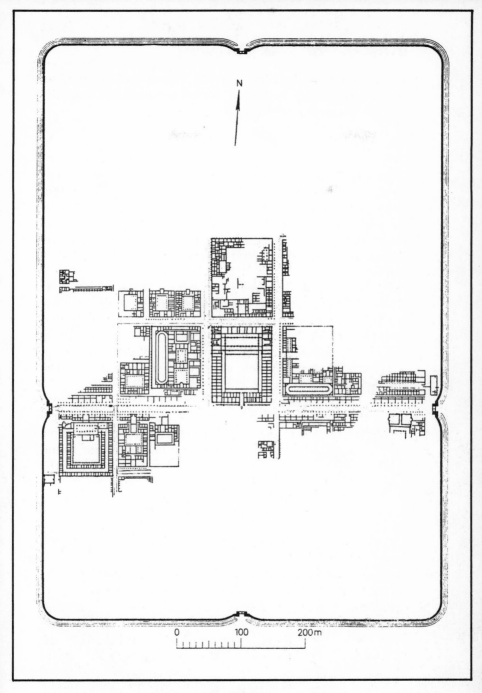

N

0      100      200m

3.4 Vetera I (Neronian), plan

basilica (for courts-martial?); the central room at the back was the shrine where the legionary standards were kept. On either side of headquarters were nearly identical mansions, each with an elliptical garden. Vetera was a camp for two legions: each commander had a house of his own. The smaller houses were for the tribunes (colonels); the enlisted men's barracks were next to the walls. Across from the west barracks was the sick bay shown in the model. The large building behind headquarters may have been the quartermaster's office.

Vetera I came to an end in blood and fire in A.D. 70, when the Batavians under Civilis captured and sacked it, slaughtering the remnant of defenders to a man, though they had been promised safe conduct. The camp had withstood a long siege, during which it was provisioned by wagon in a 1,000-man food-lift from Neuss. The rebel Civilis, who was one-eyed like Rome's old Punic enemy Hannibal, vowed not to shave off his red beard until he had defeated the Romans. In the end, the Romans outflanked and defeated him, in a battle east of the burned Vetera camp. The rebel survivors saved themselves by swimming the Rhine. A new camp, Vetera II, better protected by river and brook, was built near the site of the battle. It was discovered by skin-diving in 1958. It was for one legion only. The other had been stationed farther downstream at Noviomagus (Nymwegen; see map, Fig. 3.5), to keep a closer eye on the Batavians.

About A.D. 100, Trajan settled veterans in a walled, grid-planned colony, the Colonia Ulpia Traiana, two and a quarter miles northwest of Vetera II. A bronze bust (Fig. 3.6) found in the Rhine at Nymwegen, but apparently from Vetera, may possibly represent the founder. The trapezoidal line of the colony's circuit-wall, with its four gates and numerous towers, was traced in 1951 by electrical resistivity survey, which records where the ground has been disturbed beneath the surface.* There was also a moat,

* See *The Mute Stones Speak*, p. 46; paperback, pp. 55-56.

with "tank traps" beyond it to hinder enemy approach. Only slightly smaller than Köln, the colony became the second city of Lower Germany. An inscription records that the Rhine fleet transported stone to this sandy land to build the colony's forum. Beneath the Trajanic level the excavators hit upon remains of a native settlement of Augustan date. Just as the Ubii had been settled in what later became

**3.5 Map, lower Rhine Limes**

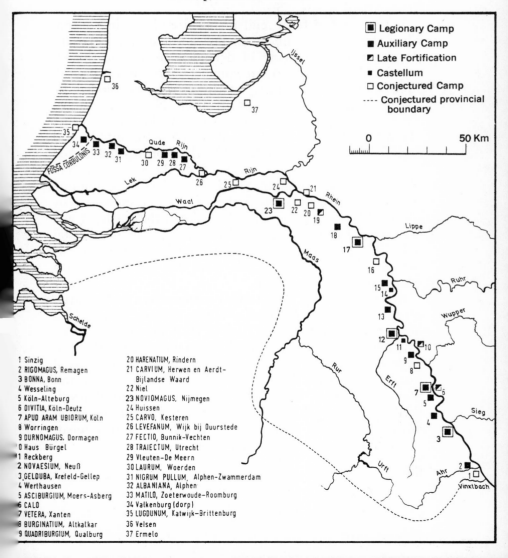

Legionary Camp
Auxiliary Camp
Late Fortification
Castellum
Conjectured Camp
---- Conjectured provincial boundary

0        50 Km

1 Sinzig
2 RIGOMAGUS, Remagen
3 BONNA, Bonn
4 Wesseling
5 Köln-Alteburg
6 DIVITIA, Köln-Deutz
7 APUD ARAM UBIORUM, Köln
8 Worringen
9 DURNOMAGUS. Dormagen
10 Haus Bürgel
11 Reckberg
12 NOVAESIUM, Neuß
13 GELDUBA, Krefeld-Gellep
14 Werthausen
15 ASCIBURGIUM, Moers-Asberg
16 CALO
17 VETERA, Xanten
18 BURGINATIUM, Altkalkar
19 QUADRIBURGIUM, Qualburg

20 HARENATIUM, Rindern
21 CARVIUM, Herwen en Aerdt-
   Bijlandse Waard
22 Niel
23 NOVIOMAGUS, Nijmegen
24 Huissen
25 CARVO, Kesteren
26 LEVEFANUM, Wijk bij Duurstede
27 FECTIO, Bunnik-Vechten
28 TRAIECTUM, Utrecht
29 Vleuten-De Meern
30 LAURUM, Woerden
31 NIGRUM PULLUM, Alphen-Zwammerdam
32 ALBANIANA, Alphen
33 MATILO, Zoeterwoude-Roomburg
34 Valkenburg (dorp)
35 LUGODUNUM, Katwijk-Brittenburg
36 Velsen
37 Ermelo

3.6 Nymwegen, bust of Trajan(?) from Vetera II

the Colonia Agrippinensis, so here the Cugerni (the name means "cowboys") had been settled in what later became the Colonia Traiana. And, in both cases, the colonial grid plan swallowed up the old settlement, nonviolently: the natives were simply absorbed into colonial life.

The colony had the usual public buildings: a Capitolium in a porticoed precinct, which contained butcher shops, perhaps having something to do with the sacrificial animals; baths; warehouse; a "palace"—or at least a mansion—with an apsidal room, and gardens; an artisans' quarter (bakery,

**68**

potter's shop, metalworkers' kilns); identical government housing, as at Trajan's Ostia, Rome's port; gravel-paved streets nearly forty feet wide, with sixteen-foot sidewalks; an aqueduct, ten of its piers revealed by World War II bombing; one of those multiple-seated latrines in which the gregarious Romans delighted; and, in the southeast corner, a modest amphitheater, only thirty-three feet high (see model, Fig. 3.7), which would seat eight to ten thousand, about one-sixth the size of the Coliseum in Rome. Bones of bears, tusks of boars, horns of bulls tell us what beasts were slaughtered here. The amphitheater was built first in wood, then, in the late second century A.D., rebuilt (the phase shown here) in stone.

The colony prospered until the 260s, when a hoard of silver coins from nearby Obladen mirrors the panic caused by a Frankish invasion at that time. But the place revived: the latest coins are dated 353. It was an early center of Christianity, and had its martyr, St. Victor, whose torture, probably in the amphitheater, made a change from bear-baiting. The modern name, Xanten, is derived from Sanctos, "saints." Legend says that Siegfried, hero of the Niebelungenlied and of Wagner's *Ring*, grew up in a nearby castle. Under Hitler, the local Siegfried Society subsidized the excavation of the amphitheater.

It will be recalled that Drusus' base for his campaigns of 10 and 9 B.C. was Moguntiacum (Mainz), named after the Celtic god Mogon, whom the Romans equated with Apollo. The site, on the left bank of the Rhine opposite the mouth of the Main, is like Vetera's opposite the Lippe. The camp (Latin *castra*) was on high ground behind the present town, an area still called Kästrich (see plan, Fig. 3.8). It was the same size as Haltern, for it, too, was designed to hold two legions. Of the Drusus camps, only Vetera was

**69**

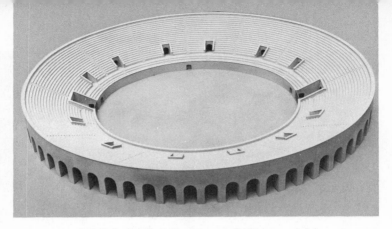

3.7  Colonia Ulpia Traiana, amphitheater, model

larger: Neuss, Bonn, Strassburg, and Windisch were all
smaller. Beside the camp, Drusus' cenotaph, the Eigelstein,
still stands over seventy feet high (plan, 5), gaunt and
stripped of its stone facing, but it is clear that it was planned
as a cylinder on a square foundation, like more famous
mausolea in Rome: Caecilia Metella's, Augustus', Hadrian's.

After the Teutoburg defeat, Mainz became the headquarters of the Roman army in Upper Germany. ("Upper"
and "Lower" refer to the upper [south] and lower [north]
reaches of the Rhine.) Sometime in the mid-first century
A.D. the camp was rebuilt in stone. The portico of the headquarters building had a balustrade, carved with reliefs, one
of which (Fig. 3.9) shows two German captives heavily
chained. They are just as Tacitus describes them, stripped
for battle, naked except for a cloak. The crude technique is
reminiscent of wood carving: the reliefs were carved in
stone to imitate originals from the camp's wood-built phase,
and it is therefore a fair inference that they commemorate
Drusus' victories.

The later camp had baths. An aqueduct served them: its
piers survive, great lumps of rubble denuded of their facing
and their arches, but still looming high enough to give impressive testimony to Roman engineering skill.

Between the camp and the river, under the modern city,
the native settlement (*canabae*) flourished, fattening, as

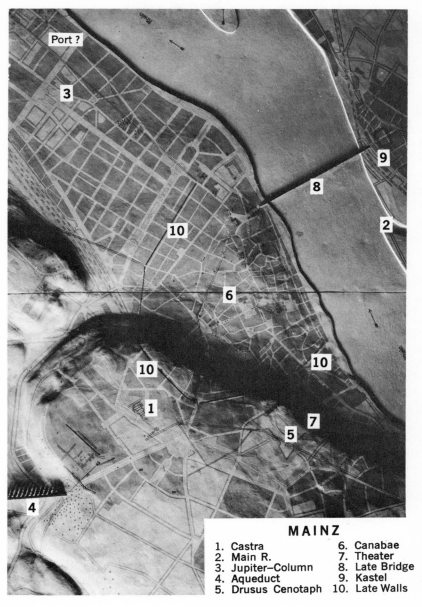

Port ?

3

9

8

2

10

6

10

10

1

7

5

4

**MAINZ**

1. Castra
2. Main R.
3. Jupiter–Column
4. Aqueduct
5. Drusus Cenotaph
6. Canabae
7. Theater
8. Late Bridge
9. Kastel
10. Late Walls

3.8 Mainz, plan

3.9 Mainz, chained German captives, relief

Rudolph Pörtner suggests, like a frontier town of the American West, on profits from the military. The grateful natives dedicated to Nero, about A.D. 65, after he had escaped assassination, a thirty-foot column surmounted by a bronze Jupiter, thunderbolt in hand, eagle at his feet. In the nineteenth century the column was found, smashed into 2,000 pieces, including the eagle and the thunderbolt, and enough of the inscription to show that Nero's name was chiseled out—in accordance with the ungrateful practice known as *damnatio memoriae*—after his suicide in 68. The double plinth and five drums that composed the column (Fig. 3.10) stand reconstructed in the Mittelrheinisches Landesmuseum in Mainz; there is a reconstruction outdoors nearby, and others at the Saalburg in the Taunus north of Frankfurt, at the museum of St.-Germain-en-Laye near Paris, and in the Museo della Civiltà Romana in Rome. The number of reproductions reflects the importance of the monument, as documenting the acceptance by provincials of the Roman official religion. The photograph reproduces a model of the column, front and back. On the front, reading from the bottom, are Jupiter and the eagle; the inscription; Victory with a palm frond; Vulcan, patron of blacksmiths; the Celtic horse-goddess Epona (of whom more in Chapter 6); the Genius of the Emperor; and Juno. On the back, Hercules with his club; Apollo with his lyre; his sister, the huntress-goddess Diana; the grain-goddess Ceres; the hearth-goddess Vesta; Liber, god of wine; and the chariot of the sun. This happy blend of native and pagan Roman elements was unsatisfactory to the early Christians: it was probably they who smashed the monument.

The Mainz legions swore allegiance to the Batavian rebels in A.D. 69, and the camp was destroyed, but immediately rebuilt in stone, for one legion only, because Domitian changed Roman strategy, making the main defense depend upon a sort of Maginot Line, the *Limes* (Fig. 3.11), to be described in the next chapter. Mainz prospered

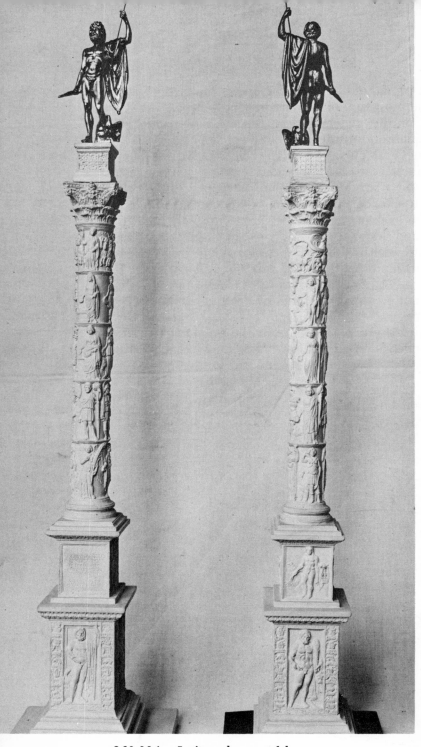

3.10  Mainz, Jupiter-column, model

as the capital of Germania Superior. One piece of evidence for the prosperity of the city under Domitian is the gravestone of the merchant Blussus—a Celtic name. He sits foursquare and sturdy in a warm woollen cloak with a cowl, holding a fat purse in his lap. His solid wife is dressed to the nines, wearing a heavy gold necklace, holding her spinning and a lap dog. Her dress has slipped coquettishly off her left shoulder: it is the only thing coquettish about her. On the back of the stone, a cargo ship with cabin, steersman, and three members of the crew suggests the source of Blussus' wealth. Villas on the east bank of the Rhine testify to Mainz' prosperity, as did a theater, as large as the Gallic ones in Arles and Orange; its remains were found (and not preserved) in building the Sudbahnhof in the last century.

Mainz' history darkens from the third century onward. Alexander Severus, the last of his dynasty, was murdered

## 3.11 Map, Limes near Mainz

| | |
|---|---|
| 1 | Heddesdorf |
| 2 | Bendorf |
| 2a | Niederberg |
| 3 | Arzbach |
| 4 | Ems |
| 5 | Hunzel |
| 5a | Marienfels |
| 6 | Holzhausen |
| 7 | Kemel |
| 8 | Zugmantel |
| 9 | Heftrich |

3.12 Mainz, Roman bridge, model

here in A.D. 235 by troops incensed at pay-cuts and a peace policy. In his place they put up—for the first time not waiting for the approval of the Senate in Rome—Maximinus the Thracian, a great ox of a man who was said to have drunk twenty-six quarts of wine and eaten forty pounds of meat a day. In 269 the soldiers murdered here the usurper Postumus, for refusing to yield the city up to sack. By the mid-fourth century, the city was walled, against constant barbarian threats: the walled area was sixty acres larger than Köln. A wooden bridge on stone piers with cutwaters (see model, Fig. 3.12) connected the city with the bridgehead *castellum* across the Rhine in the suburb still called Kastel. But walls and fortress proved unavailing against the barbarian hordes. They destroyed the city in A.D. 406, and St. Jerome records the murder of "many thousands" in the church. Mainz revived, with a mellow and humane tradition. Here the Römisch-Germanisches Zentralmuseum houses Germany's best collection of casts and copies of Roman antiquities; here Gutenberg printed the first European books, and here, in the Roman tradition, a hostelry boasts the longest list of white wines in Germany.

Though Drusus had built the camps of Haltern, Vetera, Mainz, and many others, he had, at his death, made little impression on Germany east of the Rhine. His brother

Tiberius, who succeeded him, had to leave for Pannonia with the conquest of Germany incomplete. Tiberius returned in A.D. 4, and waged two energetic campaigns, but again had to leave, this time to quell a major uprising in Illyricum (nowadays Yugoslavia). His successor, P. Quinctilius Varus, was destined to lead three Roman legions to annihilation. He had had a career in the East, but owed his preferment chiefly to the fact that he had married Augustus' grandniece. He found the Germans partially united under a faction-leader, Arminius, a Roman citizen and knight. The confrontation of Varus and Arminius has been the basis for a good deal of rhetorical writing, with Varus presented as inert or benevolent, Arminius as energetic or perfidious, depending on the bias of the author toward Rome's civilizing mission or Germany's noble-savage impulse to freedom. Bismarck, the Iron Chancellor, at the height of his career in 1875, dedicated to Arminius at Detmold a bronze statue fifty-two feet high, with a twenty-three-foot sword; a German, writing in 1934, went so far as to compare Arminius to Hitler, intending a compliment to both.

Behind the bias, it seems clear that Varus antagonized the Germans by exacting heavy tribute, drafting their young men into the army, and carrying out executions with a heavy hand. He was induced to leave his summer camp, perhaps on the upper reaches of the Lippe (see map, Fig. 3.13) by reports of uprisings eastward toward the Rhine. Encumbered with baggage, in the gumbo mud of the Teutoburg Forest, he was ambushed with three legions, XVII, XVIII, and XIX. They were all wiped out, and Varus committed suicide. Augustus in Rome dashed his head against the wall, crying, "Quinctilius Varus, give me back my legions!" The cry was in vain: the legions were never replaced, and their ill-omened numbers never used again. Official propaganda made Varus the scapegoat, branding him, in the words of Ronald Syme, as "torpid, rapacious, and incompetent."

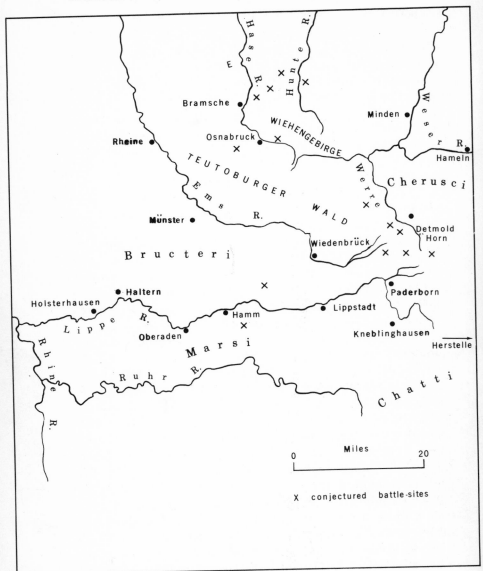

**3.13 Map, Teutoburg forest**

Though enormous quantities of ink have been spilt on the question of the precise site of the Teutoburg battle, it will probably never be known. There is no archaeological evidence: R.A.F. photographs of the area show no camp-sites, and the literary sources neither knew nor cared. The best guess is that since Drusus' son Germanicus wrought especial havoc six years later in the area between the Ems and the Lippe, the battle may have been fought there. Germanicus piously raised a mound over the whitening bones of men and horses that he found on the battlefield, and was horrified at the sight of Roman heads nailed to trees, German altars for human sacrifice, the gibbets where Roman soldiers had been hanged, and the mass graves where they had been buried.

Two specific memorials of the battle survive. One (Fig. 3.14) is the cenotaph-stone of a senior centurion of the XVIIIth, Marcus Caelius of Bologna, found near Xanten (Varus' base) in the early seventeenth century, and now in the Rheinisches Landesmuseum in Bonn. The stone records that he died "bello Variano" at the age of fifty-three. He was prosperous enough to have had two freedmen, whose busts flank his portrait on the stone. He has so many medals that they will not all fit on his breastplate: two of the seven are visible behind his shoulders. He wears the civic crown of oak leaves, awarded for saving the life of a fellow-Roman.

The other possible memorial of the battle is a treasure consisting of eighty pieces of an elegant silver service for three, weighing nearly 120 pounds, found at Hildesheim, some eighty miles east of the probable battleground, by soldiers building a rifle range in 1868. Part of the treasure is a handsome silver punch bowl (Fig. 3.15) embellished with Cupids fishing, stylized plants, and griffins, now on display with the rest of the treasure in the Pelizaeus Museum in Hildesheim. The argument, which does not convince all scholars, is that only a high-ranking Roman officer like Varus could have possessed so elegant a service, that it

3.14 Bonn, cenotaph of Caelius, killed with Varus

represents Arminius' share of the booty, buried and never recovered, for Arminius was betrayed and killed in A.D. 17. The pieces were made in Pergamum, North Africa, and Syria: Varus had served in all these places. One piece, bearing the name of one Marcus Scato, governor of the Roman province of Crete and Cyrene before 12 B.C., may have been presented or sold to Varus. The name Marcus Aurelius, on another piece, need not be so late as the philosopher-Emperor (A.D. 161-180): the name occurs also in the early Empire, in Varus' time. Finally, only at the time of the Teutoburg battle, it is alleged, could Germans have got their hands on this much booty.

The opposition argues that the collection is a mixed bag, including a number of provincial pieces, not fit for an officer, much of it not made till after Varus was dead. Since each piece is stamped with the name of a different owner, the collection is more likely to have been made by a Roman merchant for sale to newly rich Germans. While finality is impossible, the weight of the evidence seems to be on the side of those who see the Hildesheim treasure as belonging to Varus.

The Teutoburg disaster was decisive. Rome postponed, and finally renounced the conquest of Germany between the Rhine and the Elbe. Augustus in his will (A.D. 14) advised his successor Tiberius and his fellow Romans "to be satisfied with the status quo and to suppress completely any desire to increase the Empire to greater size." Tiberius heeded the advice. An important piece of archaeological evidence that he did so is the seventy-two-acre legionary camp of Vindonissa (Windisch), first built in his reign, in A.D. 15 or 16, on a spur between rivers in Switzerland, just south of the Rhine and east of Augst, controlling road and river traffic at a discreet distance from the barbarian

3.15  Hildesheim treasure: silver wine bowl

tribes across the Rhine to the north. The model (Fig. 3.16)
shows the camp in its stone-built phase, between A.D. 46
and 70, equipped with the same types of major buildings as
Xanten: headquarters (1), sick bay (2), arsenal (3), barracks (4), baths (5), and tribunes' quarters (6). Since the
model was made, two other buildings, both warehouses,
have been excavated at (7) and (8). Immediately to the
southwest, just off the upper left corner of the photograph,
was the forum of the civilian settlement, and, still farther
southwest, the amphitheater.

The most interesting aspect of Vindonissa was its rubbish
dump, just beyond the north gate (Fig. 3.16, top right). It
was found in laying out the railway line in 1855, and dug
by patients from the local insane asylum, one of whom
proved that one does not have to be sane to be fascinated
by archaeology: he ran off with a box of baubles, and had
to be brought back by the police. This gigantic kitchen-
midden contained oyster shells, peach and plum pits, hazel-
nuts, chestnuts; amphoras that once contained oil, beans,
and the much-prized fish sauce called *garum*.* There is a
particularly fine collection of safety pins (*fibulae*) of the
first century A.D. (Fig. 3.17). Conditions were ideal for the

* See *The Iberian Stones Speak*, pp. 207-209.

preservation of leather and wood: the soles of hobnailed boots, pierced leatherwork, combs and brushes (Fig. 3.18), shingles, window-frames, and poles of oak and fir (which may have been the wooden tracks on which the rubbish carts were wheeled out to the edge of the dump. Others think they are the remains of the camp palisade, thrown away when a stone circuit-wall replaced it after a fire about A.D. 50). A number of wooden writing tablets still bore legible messages on the wax. One intriguing one reads, "Deliver to Belice opposite the Baths. I'll come tomorrow at dawn before I go to the villa. Even if I leave before daylight, I'm afraid I'll be recognized. Please send my hobnailed boots . . ." These finds are on display in the nearby town of Brugg, in the Vindonissa Museum, whose entrance is designed as a full-sized reproduction of one of the camp gates.

Camps like Vindonissa gave the Romans bases for commercial expansion in towns, eastward into Raetia. One such town is Brigantium, on the eastern end of Lake Constance (nowadays Bregenz, just over the Swiss border in Austria). It is at an important road junction: southward over

**3.16 Vindonissa, camp, model**

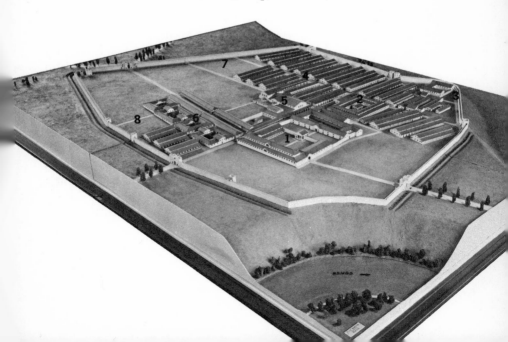

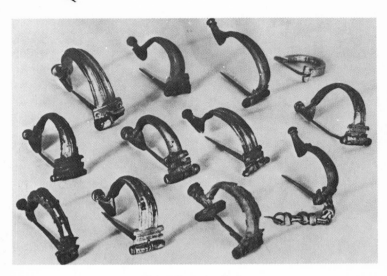

3.17 Vindonissa, *fibulae*

the Alps to Milan, northeastward into the Danube valley. The buildings of the town are strung out, not on a grid plan, on a terrace overlooking the lake, along the road to Raetia (Fig. 3.19) There are villas, baths, shops, offices, warehouses, a post-house, a forum with heated offices arranged around a square, and a Capitolium, at the head of the road to Milan. There was also a *castellum* for a small detachment of troops, and a naval station on the lake, which between them apparently supplied all necessary security, for the town had no circuit-wall. It is dated by dedications to Drusus. Under Claudius (A.D. 41-54) it became a *municipium*; i.e., it had local self-government. Such status indicated a feeling on the part of the authorities in Rome that a native town had become Romanized enough to be trusted.

Thirty miles northeast of Brigantium, on the Raetian road, was Cambodunum (nowadays Kempten, in Bavaria). Germanicus left a garrison here when Tiberius recalled him, after indecisive campaigns, in A.D. 17. The garrison moved forward to the Danube under Claudius (A.D. 46-47). The civil population stayed, their civic center more than usually elegant, being stone-built from the first, in order to impress the local peoples with Roman sophistication. They must have been impressed as well with the severity of Roman law: in a cemetery of the first century A.D., one of the skeletons found had its hands tied; he must have been a condemned criminal. Plan and models of the buildings are on display in the Zumsteinhaus on the other side of the river Iller in the medieval town. One of the curiosities of the museum is a curse-tablet, inscribed as usual on lead, expressing the pious hope that the object of the curse "may run about frantic like a fleeing mouse" ("agitatus erret ut mus fugiens"). Since Kempten is now a dairying center, the excavator's report that 63 percent of the ancient animal bones found were of cows is of interest, as is also the discovery of a number of ancient cow-bells. Sixty percent of the public area was taken up by a huge (780 x 583-foot)

**3.18 Vindonissa, Schutthügel: leatherwork, comb, brush**

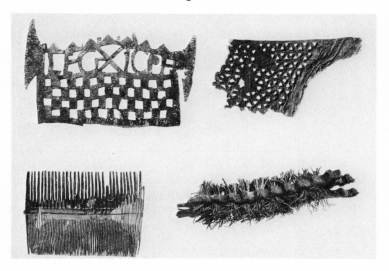

**3.19 Brigantium, plan**

temple precinct, as large as Palmyra's; * it was probably
dedicated to Rome and Augustus. It has now been largely
destroyed by a gravel pit. Adjoining it on the northwest was
the forum, with curia and basilica; there were also two sets
of public baths. The dimensions of the forum are exactly

* See *The Greek Stones Speak*, p. 408; paperback, p. 372.

preserved in the courtyard of a new school next door.

But the most exceptional building in Cambodunum was the hotel (Fig. 3.20) just north of the forum. The model shows it as rebuilt after the fire of 69-70. It had over fifty rooms, two annexes, and two courts, in which vehicles could be parked. Its second-floor rooms had balconies, and it conveniently adjoins the smaller of the public baths and an exercise-ground.

The hotel stood through the prosperous years of the second century, but, like so much else in Roman Germany, was destroyed in the barbarian invasion of A.D. 260, after which the few remaining settlers moved to the other side of the river, where modern Kempten stands. Bronze hoofs of horses, from ruined equestrian statues, found in the ruins of the forum, bear mute testimony to the havoc the barbarians wrought.

Fifty miles north-northwest of Kempten, at Oberhausen, Drusus built a legionary camp. Under Tiberius' status quo policy, the garrison was withdrawn to Vindonissa in A.D. 15, but the site became commercially important under the name of Augusta Vindelicum, nowadays Augsburg, the terminus of the Via Claudia Augusta from Italy, the capital of the province of Raetia, and the seat of the Roman procurator. Since the Roman town lies under a flourishing modern city of 200,000, it cannot be completely excavated, but the present cathedral marks roughly its center. Just to

**3.20 Cambodunum, hotel, reconstruction**

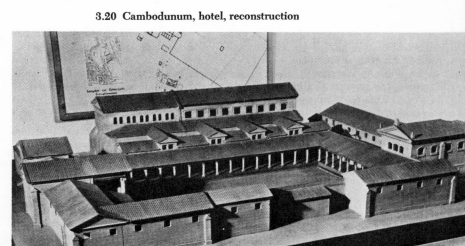

the south is a peristyle house; there are Roman baths in the Georgenstrasse to the north, and one of the Roman gates in the Heilig-Kreuzstrasse to the west. In the Römisches Museum, handsomely housed in a deconsecrated Dominican church, a relief (Fig. 3.21) of a workman baling wool under the watchful eye of a clerk reminds us of Augsburg's continuing commercial importance: wool was the foundation of the fortune of the millionaire Fuggers, Augsburg citizens who subsidized the Hapsburgs in the sixteenth century.

The present capital of West Germany owes its foundation to Drusus. In Bonn (Bonna) there are Roman graves under the Parliament building, a Roman kiln under the White House. Pliny the Elder wrote part of his encyclopedia and his *German Wars* here, and Beethoven was born within a half mile of the Roman camp. The finds, of which more turn up every day, e.g., enough Roman coins to pay a legion, are handsomely housed in the new (1969) building of the oldest Roman museum in Germany, the Rheinisches Landesmuseum in the Colmantstrasse, founded in 1876.

Drusus' was a bridgehead camp (remains under the Minoritenplatz); in its Claudian phase (A.D. 41-54) the Roman camp lay north of the present Beethovenhalle, between the Rhine and the Kaiser-Karl-Ring; the Koblenz-Köln highway follows the line of its *Via Principalis*. The chief curiosities of the camp are a horse-hospital, and a building variously identified in the past as a dressing room, a barracks, a pigsty, or a columbarium (for cremation-urns). It turns out to have been the military prison, or brig. Quarters in the camp were cramped. When one considers a twenty-year hitch spent in the leaden monotony of barracks crowded, unheated, and badly lit, the wonder is not

3.21 Augsburg, workman tying a bale, relief

that the legions mutinied, but that they were so loyal: one of the Bonn legions was nicknamed Pia Fidelis, "Old Faithful." In any case it is no wonder that they welcomed war. Parades on the Emperor's birthday, or beast-fights in the amphitheater, relieved peacetime tedium. And by the late second century, under the Severan dynasty, an old-fashioned centurion like Caelius would feel grounds for saying the army was being spoiled: no longer a distinction between officers and men, Levantine and frontier barbarian recruits, baths and mosaics in the camps, soldiers allowed to live with their women (or their men: a Bonn inscription in Greek verse was written by a man in love with a eunuch).

Another famous city that owed its foundation to Tiberius' retrenchment policy was Strassburg, which the Romans called Argentorate. As a camp, it lasted till Claudius withdrew its legion in A.D. 43 to help in his invasion of Britain. As elsewhere, a civilian settlement filled the gap left by the legion: its forum was in the present Cathedral square. The town was burned in the Batavian uprising, and a legion was quartered there again from A.D. 70, but the place lost its military importance when Domitian (A.D. 81-96) pushed the frontier eastward across the Rhine to the far side of the Neckar valley. But Strassburg still had commercial value as a river port. In the fourth century A.D. the area between the Cathedral and the moat from the river Ill was walled, the walls, in shape, area, and towers much like the late walls of Barcelona.* This citadel was too small to hold the civilian population comfortably, but perhaps in an emergency it could be crowded in. That emergency came about A.D. 450, when the Roman town was wiped out, but Strassburg survived as a Frankish settlement: the oldest part of the Cathedral, famous for its lofty towers, dates from 1015.

At Novaesium, nowadays Neuss, on the west bank of the Rhine between Köln and Xanten, there were three successive camps in Augustus' reign, one of which must have been the work of Drusus. But the one about which we know most was built under Tiberius, in the 30s A.D. It covered sixty acres, and was protected by a moat thirty-three feet wide and ten feet deep. It had the usual careful grid plan, and the usual buildings, with which we have become familiar at Xanten and Windisch. It was the scene, during the Batavian uprising, of a double disgrace, more damaging to Roman honor than the Teutoburg disaster: the legionaries murdered their commanding officer, and swore an oath of allegiance to the rebels. The camp, together with those at Vetera and Bonn, was destroyed. Cerialis, the Roman general who put down the rebellion, rebuilt the camp, adding twelve watchtowers and four gates with dual carriageways; the principal buildings were now faced with tufa and stuccoed.

West of the camp, over the ruins of the Augustan fortifications, the *canabae* sprang up, on an extension of the Via *Principalis*. The settlement's long, narrow wooden buildings, their narrow ends facing the street, contained pottery

* See *The Iberian Stones Speak*, pp. 198-217.

kilns, a coppersmith's shop, and a tannery. The Roman army consumed goods in wholesale quantities, and supplying them was a profitable business. In the Neuss *canabae* was found, after World War II, the silvered copper helmet in Figure 3.22. It looks as if it were used for playing polo, but the projection is not a visor but a neck-protector, with a hole bored through it for slinging it round the neck on the march. The knob on top was for attaching the crest, and there are knobs on the sides for fastening on the cheek-pieces. Another recent find, from a grave, is a heavy rock-crystal ring (Fig. 3.23), engraved with the figure of Mars, holding a Corinthian helmet, and carrying lance and shield. Such rings were believed to cool hellfire. Altogether, over 200,000 recent finds await cataloguing.

The military and civil settlements of Neuss survived the invasions of A.D. 260, but on a reduced scale. Julian the Apostate, in 359, before he became Emperor, emulated Drusus by building camps on the Rhine, seven of them, including Neuss. There is continuity at Neuss: the oldest medieval settlement is on the site of the latest Roman one.

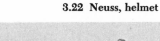

**3.22  Neuss, helmet**

3.23 Neuss, rock crystal ring

We have seen how a revolt in Pannonia kept Tiberius occupied from A.D. 6 to 9. Since he had personally pacified it, he had no intention, when he came to the throne, of letting it slip from Roman hands under his predecessor's recommended status quo policy. Therefore, in A.D. 15, he built in its extreme northern part, at Carnuntum, on the Danube between Deutsch-Altenburg and Petronell, about twenty-five miles east of Vindobona (present-day Vienna) a legionary fortress that in antiquity was far more important than the present capital of Austria. Carnuntum, situated as it was at the crossing of the Danube-valley road and the amber route from the Baltic, controlled the no man's land the Romans created for five miles either side of the Danube, but it had commercial as well as military importance: just southwest of the camp there flourished in the early Empire a typical Roman provincial frontier town. In A.D. 106 Trajan made it the capital of Upper Pannonia. Hadrian made it a *municipium*; the philosopher-Emperor Marcus

Aurelius wrote part of his famous *Meditations* here; Septimius Severus, who was serving here as governor when he received news of his accession to the throne (A.D. 193), elevated it to the status of colony.

The forty-two-acre camp conforms to the canonical plan already seen at Vetera, Vindonissa, and Novaesium; like Vindonissa, it had a forum just to the southwest, and, outdoing Vetera and Vindonissa, it had not one amphitheater but two: one just northeast of the camp, the other, larger (it would hold 13,000) just south of the town. A unique feature of the camp was a tunnel for emergency exits. In the armory was found one of the triple-pointed objects the soldiers called "crow's-feet": no matter how it was thrown, one point always fell uppermost, to hinder approach to the wall. In the grain store were bins of carbonized barley, which, had it not been burned, would have been used for making beer. A room with a vaulted wine-cooler, an altar to the wine-god, quantities of broken drinking-cups, and half of a pair of dice, has been plausibly taken to be the centurion's mess. The amphitheater had a tunnel through which dead gladiators might be dragged to be thrown into the Danube. The camp was covered over again after excavation, and archaeological work in the town was interrupted by World War II (though Hitler ordered the whole of it unearthed); the job is still only one-third completed. The finds, from camp and town, are on display in the fine Deutsch-Altenburg museum. In the town, half of a sumptuous palace, probably the governor's, has been unearthed. It overlooks the Danube, as the one in Köln overlooks the Rhine. It measured 341 x 469 feet (about one hundred times the area of an average American house); its thick walls show that it had more than one story. It had radiant heating, window glass, and rooms veneered with Greek and Syrian marble. Coins show it was in its prime in the second century A.D.: Marcus Aurelius may have slept here.

Southeast of the palace three blocks of the town have been preserved as an out-of-door museum (Fig. 3.24). It is

a prosperous artisans' quarter with simple but bright-colored
—even loud—wall decoration, including a dancer bearing
an uncanny resemblance to film-star Elizabeth Taylor.
South of the houses, across the Vienna highway, rises the
Heidentor, the only pagan structure above ground in Austria
(Fig. 3.25). It was originally a four-sided arch, erected to
celebrate a triumph of Constantius II (A.D. 337-361).

The road to Italy runs east of the Heidentor. It is bordered with tombs, one of which yielded a rolled silver
plaque inscribed ABLATANABLA SABAOTH. It is a charm
against migraine, believed to be brought on by a female
sea demon who mooed like a cow. The graves in the cemetery run down into the late fourth century. Shortly thereafter, Carnuntum fell, in a sudden catastrophe: skeletons
were found in the streets of the town, and in the camp
bakery there was a loaf of bread still in the oven.

The boundary line between the Roman provinces of
Pannonia and Noricum (Austria) ran just west of Carnuntum. The Romanization of Noricum is due chiefly to
Claudius (reigned A.D. 41-54). He founded Juvavum (Salzburg, Mozart's city), the Danube camp Lauriacum (Lorch:
see Chapter 4), Aguntum (Lienz, in the east Tyrol),
Teurnia (St. Peter in Holz, in Carinthia), and Virunum
(Zollfeld, near Klagenfurt), the capital of the province, with
a fascinating mining town on the Magdalensberg towering

3.24 Carnuntum, artisans' quarter (open-air museum)

3.25 Carnuntum, Heidentor

above it. Vespasian founded Flavia Solva, as a purely civilian settlement, with a strong Celtic strain in the population, as names on an inscription show. It was destroyed in the Marcomannic War, but rebuilt on a grid plan (see model, Fig. 3.26). It had a forum (model, center), and an amphitheater with a walled farmstead beside it like Köln-Müngersdorf. This phase lasted till about A.D. 405, when the barbarians destroyed it. All the towns except Salzburg are off the beaten tourist track, and well worth a visit.

For a man who in his lifetime bore a reputation (undeserved) for stupidity, Claudius was an extraordinarily energetic imperialist. After the Chatti had destroyed (A.D. 51) a fort built against them by Caligula in A.D. 39 or 40 at Hofheim in the Taunus mountains between Frankfurt and Wiesbaden, Claudius rebuilt it, and it was garrisoned till Vespasian moved the frontier forward in the 70s. The camp is a landmark for archaeologists, because especially careful excavation here made it possible to set up a typology of finds of *fibulae* and pottery (the datable kind called

**95**

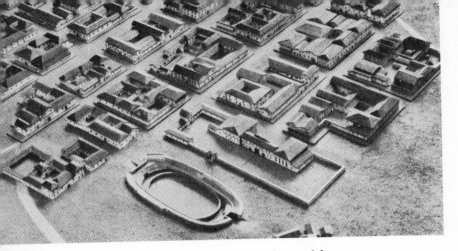

3.26 Flavia Solva, model

*terra sigillata*, stamped with makers' marks), which has been invaluable in dating of other sites.

Another Claudian camp, at Valkenburg at the very mouth of the Rhine in south Holland, is of great interest because it was the base for Claudius' invasion of Britain in A.D. 42. A model excavation has distinguished six phases. Noteworthy is the special construction necessitated by the Dutch terrain (Fig. 3.27): a corduroy road runs round the camp just inside the wall, and the barracks are built on a special wooden grid supported by deep-driven piles. Despite precautions, the camp was flooded by the first spring tides, and had to be rebuilt. Pirates destroyed it in 47; it was again rebuilt. The Batavians burned it in 70; it was rebuilt a third time. The fifth phase is due to Trajan's engineers, about A.D. 100, the final phase to Septimius Severus' (reigned A.D. 193-211). It was finally abandoned about A.D. 250.

The sites described so far in this chapter were foundations of the Julio-Claudian Emperors: Augustus, Tiberius, Caligula, Claudius. (Nero had little interest in Germany.)

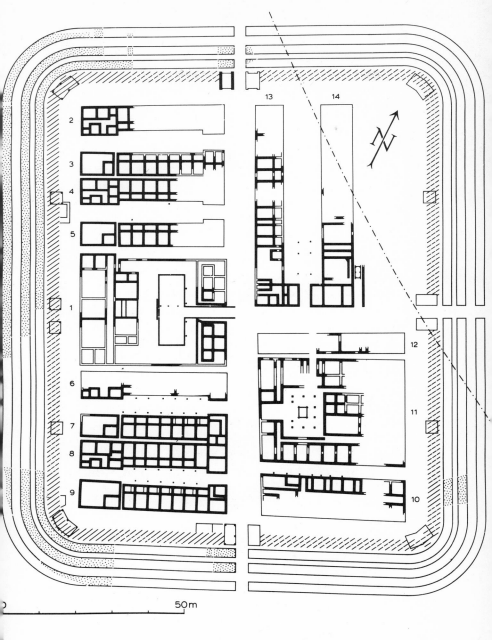

3.27 Valkenburg, Roman camp, partial plan

97

After the unrest of the Four Emperors' Year (A.D. 69) which followed Nero's suicide, Vespasian, founder of a new, bourgeois dynasty, the Flavian, emerged victorious. He founded for his veterans (A.D. 73 or 74) the last city to be discussed in this chapter, Colonia Pia Flavia Constans Emerita Helvetiorum Foederata Aventicum (nowadays, with merciful brevity, Avenches), just south of Lake Neuchâtel. It was surrounded, apparently from the beginning, with a huge, seventy-three-towered wall, three and a half miles in circumference (Fig. 3.28). A part of the walled area was laid out with the standard Roman grid; the rest was left unbuilt, as a place of refuge for surrounding farmers, with their flocks and herds, in case of emergency. Avenches had the usual amenities: baths, an amphitheater seating 15,000, which survives, with a museum adjoining. Between the amphitheater and the town grid, a theater, for 9,000, faces a temple at the back of a rectangular precinct, as at Augst. Only one column of the temple survives, called, for obvious reasons, the Stork's Nest (Le Cigognier). In the temple drain was found a bust of Marcus Aurelius in 22-carat gold, about a foot high. It was concealed there at the threat of invasion, perhaps in A.D. 260;

**3.28 Avenches, Roman wall and tower**

**3.29  Avenches, she-wolf and twins, relief**

its owner probably did not live to recover it. Another find, also in the museum, is a relief in the style of the first century A.D., depicting the foundation legend of Rome itself: the she-wolf suckling the royal twins Romulus and Remus, the founders of the Eternal City (Fig. 3.29).

This provincial work, set up in a Roman colony soon after its foundation, symbolizes the desire of the colonists to identify themselves loyally with Rome, her history and her culture. This is evidence that the enterprise with which this chapter has been concerned was a success; the military camps did their job, and were either abandoned or developed into cities: Xanten, Mainz, Bregenz, Kempten, Augsburg, Bonn, Straussburg, and the others. The Teutoburg disaster caused Rome to draw in her horns, but not to withdraw altogether from the work of Romanization. Behind the self-imposed limits of her retrenchment, Rome was turning frontier posts into small replicas of Italian cities on German soil.

The next step was to protect these cities by fortifying a permanent frontier, the *Limes*. The story of this frontier will be told in the next chapter.

**99**

# 4 : *The Wide Frontier*

THE most portentous landmark of the Roman occupation of Germany is the Limes (pronounced "leé-mess"), a frontier line that runs for 330 miles, from the Rhine at Vinxtbach below Sinzig to the Danube at Eining above Regensburg (see maps, Figs. 4.1 and 4.15). It is natural to think at once of the analogy of the Berlin Wall, but the analogy is false. The function of the Roman Limes was not to keep Roman subjects in, but to keep barbarians out; or rather not even that: simply to control their passage upon their lawful occasions. And there was nothing particularly formidable about the Limes: for years it was nothing but a wickerwork fence, with earthwork forts and wooden signal-towers at intervals. Hadrian (A.D. 117-138) made it a continuous wooden palisade (Fig. 4.2); Antoninus Pius (A.D. 138-161) rebuilt the forts in stone; Caracalla (A.D. 211-217) added a ditch; and only under him was a wall of stone built, and then only on the Raetian Limes (Fig. 4.3). The army lay in fancied security behind the Limes, like the French in World War II behind the Maginot Line. And, like the Maginot Line, the Limes did not hold: the barbarians pierced it in A.D. 260, and the Romans again, as after Teutoburg 250 years before, were forced to draw in their horns.

A trip along the Limes can be extremely rewarding, not so much because of the visible remains, which are much less well preserved than Hadrian's Wall in Britain, but because the charming, unspoiled country through which the Limes runs is off the beaten tourist track, and has

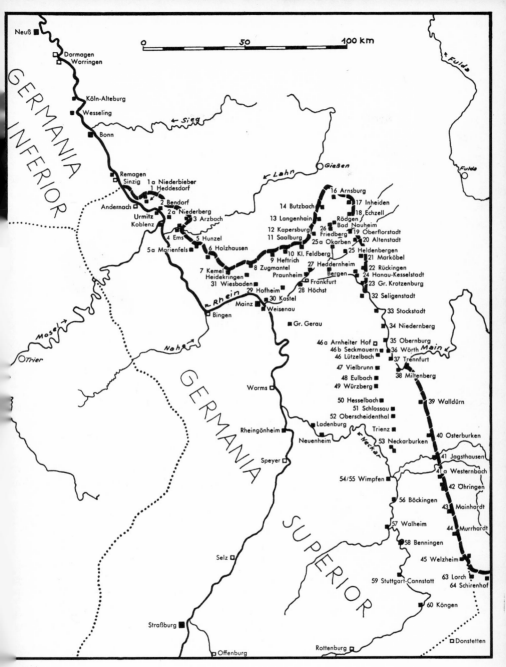

**4.1 Map, upper German Limes**

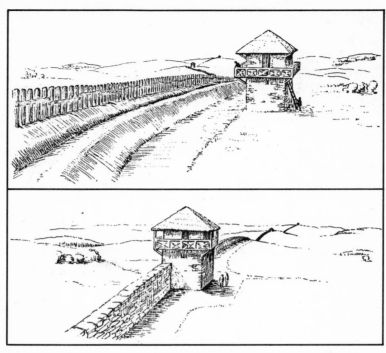

4.2  Upper German Limes, Hadrianic palisade and tower, sketch

4.3  Raetian Limes, Caracallan stone wall and tower, sketch

changed little since Roman times. A typical stretch, in the
Taunus near the Saalburg, is illustrated in Figure 4.4. The
line of the Limes is not even very easy to get at. As in
Roman times, roads usually run not along it, but up to it;
the major Roman highways, which the modern ones follow,
ran well behind the Limes line. The explorer of the Limes
can understand the excitement with which William Cam-
den wrote, in 1599, of the other Limes in Britain: "I have
seene the tract of it over the high pitches and steepe de-
scents of hilles, wonderfully rising and falling." The difficulty of access is itself a challenge, and there are a number
of sites, on which we shall concentrate, with visible remains
that are well worth the effort of visiting.

The line of the Limes has been investigated, and published with typical German thoroughness in fourteen stout volumes. Interest in modern times began in 1748, when the Prussian Academy of Sciences, in the reign of Frederick the Great, offered a prize for the best study of how far the Romans penetrated beyond the Rhine and the Danube. But the real impetus began a century and more later, when German nationalism, represented by the great historian Theodor Mommsen, by Moltke, and by Bismarck, agreed that a united Germany must protect Germany's oldest historical monument from further inroads. The government made an initial grant of 200,000 marks, and state and local historical societies collaborated, taking responsibility for the various stretches into which the Limes was divided for survey and publication. The professional competence of the local archaeologists in charge varied widely; it was part-time work, often left for days on end to unsupervised workmen. But the final publication, uneven as it is, is a monument in itself to methodical German patience. It records seventy-five major *castella*, and over 1,000 intervening watchtowers. Several of the major forts are of more than ordinary interest, and these I propose to describe, proceeding along the Limes from north to south.

4.4 Limes in Taunus, typical stretch, with ditch and earthwork

The showplace of the Limes is the Saalburg (map, Fig. 4.1, No. 11). Conveniently reached from Frankfurt, or from the nearby casino and spa of Bad Homburg, it is annually visited by 200,000 people, particularly on Sundays, which are therefore to be avoided. It is a showplace because it was completely restored, between 1898 and 1907, by Kaiser Wilhelm II, intent on underlining his fancied resemblance to the fort-building Caesars whose name he bore. The reconstruction, shown in the air-view, Figure 4.5, presents the fort as it was in its early-third-century stone phase. All the reconstructed buildings rest on genuine Roman foundations, but much of the detail in the superstructure is copied from the Roman fort best known in 1898, at Lambaesis in North Africa. From Lambaesis, by the way, comes an inscription in which Hadrian praises the troops for their alacrity in camp-building. It presents an expert's appreciation of the amount of labor that went into building forts like the Saalburg, in either its earthwork (under Domitian, *ca.* A.D. 90) or its stone-wood phase (Hadrianic, *ca.* A.D. 130, measuring 482 x 725 feet, to accommodate 500 men). It reads in part:

⟨[ *Trenches which others would have taken several days to dig, you finished in a day. You built a difficult wall, fit for permanent quarters, in not much longer than it takes to build one of turf. Turf is cut to uniform size, is easy to carry and handle, and not hard to lay, being naturally soft and even. But you used big, heavy stones of odd sizes, hard to carry, lift, and set. You have cut a straight moat through hard, coarse gravel, and leveled it off . . .*

The 1898 interpretation of the result of such labors, however instructive to look at, somehow looks more like Wilhelmine architecture than like Roman, as is made clear in the photograph of the main gate (Fig. 4.6), where not only the architecture, but also the inscription—to Wilhelm II—

**4.5  Saalburg, air view**

and the statue—of Antoninus Pius—are modern. The bridge crosses a double ditch: not a moat, for it was never filled with water. The original fort would have had the stonework stuccoed, and the crenellations farther apart. The stucco would have made the north gate (seen from within in Fig. 4.7) look less quaintly like a Swiss chalet. And we now know that in the headquarters building, visible in the center of the air-photograph, as a concession to the bleak winter climate, the smaller second court would have been not open but roofed.

The air-photograph also shows the ground-plans of two buildings outside the main gate. The *mansio* was an inn for travelers on official business: to minister to the comfort of thin-blooded Italians, the rooms were centrally heated. In the closely adjoining baths, larger than those in most Roman small towns, we have, leading from the entrance on the inn side, a long, narrow dressing room, with a latrine in the corner abutting on the inn; a steam room and a cold pool, side by side; then two warm pools, the first apsidal, for tubs; beyond, the hot pool, also apsidal; and the furnace room. The baths had window glass, walls richly painted within and stuccoed white without, and a red tile roof.

4.6 Saalburg, main gate

The fort's granary, to the right of the Via Principalis, just inside the main gate, now serves as a museum, which exhibits the greatest variety of objects of a soldier's daily life to be seen in any museum in Germany: among many other things, there are axes, hammers, planes, keys, tiles made in local kilns. The ninety-nine wells inside and outside the fort have yielded, like the rubbish dump at Vindonissa, objects of wood and leather, well preserved through being sealed off from the air. An example is the shoe in Figure 4.8: too highly decorated for a soldier, it must have belonged to a woman who lived in the *canabae* outside the wall and had a soldier for bedmate. There is much pottery: lamps; and both the elegant red polished and embossed *terra sigillata* tableware, made from molds, in imitation of more expensive silver services, and plain ware used for cooking. There are surgical instruments, writing styluses and tablets, brooches with enamel inlay, glassware, coins (3,250 were found: Roman clothes had no pockets). Behind the granary two barracks have been reconstructed in wood. Opposite it, across the Via Principalis, is the camp commander's office.

The Via Principalis leads to the central headquarters building, which contains a number of interesting working models of Roman mechanical weapons, such as crossbows. The rooms around the court, once the armory, now contain finds from pre-Roman sites near the Saalburg. The central room at the back of the second court was the shrine for the standards, and the statue of the reigning Emperor, in the late Empire often made with a detachable head, for Emperors come and Emperors go, but marble is expensive. The shrine now contains inscriptions, and copies of statues of Hadrian, who first built the fort in stone, and Severus Alexander (reigned A.D. 222-235), who was the reigning Emperor in the phase of the fort here reconstructed. The adjoining rooms were offices. Around the headquarters building run traces of the ditch of the smaller earthwork fort that preceded the reconstructed version: the whole fort was scarcely larger than the headquarters building of the later phase. It would hold a detachment of about 120 men. The bath-building to the north is oriented with, and therefore belonged to, the earthwork camp.

The Limes (black line on model, Fig. 4.9) runs only 200 yards north of the Saalburg fort. In the other direction, south of the main gate, stretch the *canabae*, the native village. The foundations of the long, narrow wooden houses survive: they were pubs, workshops, and dwellings. Beyond them, still farther south, the model shows, in black, the outline of shrines to two Near Eastern deities much venerated by the soldiers: Cybele, the Mother Goddess, from Asia Minor, and Mithras, the Persian god of light. We shall discuss them further in Chapter 6. Still farther south, beyond the shrines, was the cemetery.

**4.7 Saalburg, north gate**

Beyond the Saalburg the Limes turns northwestward. Near Butzbach, beyond the American housing development east of the town, a wooden watchtower with balcony and thatched roof has been accurately reconstructed (Fig. 4.10). In this stretch the Limes forms a deep salient, following the 200-meter contour-line of the Taunus. At Echzell (Fig. 4.1, No. 18), where it turns south again, recent careful excavation has revealed officers' quarters with wall-paintings. Such luxury does not square with the stereotype of austerity associated with military barracks, but at the time the walls were painted, in the mid-second century A.D., the army was being pampered, and we should probably have much more evidence of such decoration elsewhere if the fragile fragments had been more carefully noted by earlier excavators. The technique is not fresco but secco, using a quick-drying casein-base paint that requires of the artist great speed and dexterity. The artist was competent but not great; he used chiaroscuro and strong color contrast. There are three mythological scenes. Theseus beats the Minotaur with a shepherd's crook; Daedalus with a hammer adjusts Icarus' right wing, which is bound to his arm

**4.8  Saalburg, woman's shoe**

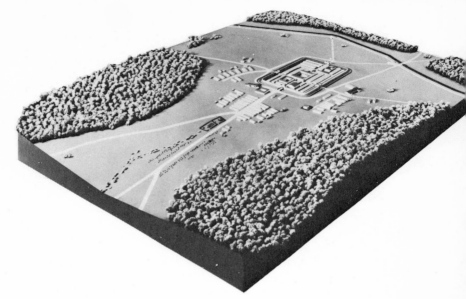

**4.9 Saalburg, model**

with straps. To underline Daedalus' reputation as a craftsman (besides being the world's first aviator, he built the
labyrinthine palace of King Minos of Crete), there is a saw
leaning against the cliff. The central scene, about ten feet
long, is of Hercules and Fortune, against a blue-gray background. Hercules is naked, with club, bow, and lion-skin.
Fortune carries her wheel, and a horn of plenty: she is
dressed in violet, with a yellow-green cloak. Both figures
wear laurel crowns. This is work on a level considerably
above that of most modern wallpaper. This reminiscence of
Graeco-Roman culture in the northern wilds has something
touching and pathetic about it, like scenes from home on
the walls of an officers' club in a British colonial outpost.

From Echzell to Seligenstadt the Limes runs south to the
Main: west of it, the industrial suburbs of Frankfurt; eastward, the delectable woodlands of the Spessart. At Seligenstadt it meets the Main, which served as the frontier: the
forts continue, but not the palisade. From the east corner
of the Stockstadt *castellum* (33) was published in 1963 a

4.10 Butzbach, reconstructed watch-tower

remarkably large coin hoard (Fig. 4.11), 6 rare gold coins
and 1,315 silver *denarii*. The last coins in it were minted
midway in Marcus Aurelius' reign; the panic that caused
them to be buried is plausibly connected with a raid of the
Chatti in A.D. 170. The hoard suggests, as usual, that the
Limes proved inadequate to keep off the barbarians in fear
of whom the hoard had been buried. It is now in the
Aschaffenburg museum. A Stockstadt inscription shows
that the fort was manned by *beneficiarii*—road police—
functioning more as customs officers than as soldiers. This
emphasizes the function of the Limes as economic as well
as military.

At Wörth (36) the Limes splits into an eastern and a
western branch. The evidence is that the western line, the
Odenwald Limes, is the older: the forts first built under
Domitian about A.D. 90, and abandoned about 148, when
Antoninus Pius pushed the line forward to the stretch,
string-straight after Miltenberg for fifty miles, which runs
from Walldürn (39) to Welzheim (45).

On the western stretch, in the rich, unspoiled field and
forest country of the Odenwald, the greatest curiosity is
Eulbach (48). The fort lay in the property of Count Franz
von Erbach-Erbach (1754-1823), a mighty hunter and connoisseur of the romantic pleasures of ruins. He excavated
the fort himself, and, from numbered stones, reconstructed

its gate in an English garden he built (1802-1807) adjoining his hunting lodge, and tenanted with animals. The garden also contains another gate, from the nearby *castellum* of Würzberg (49), and an obelisk built from stones, some of them inscribed, from the same place. He also restored the camp baths at Würzberg, but was content to leave them *in situ*. There are also inscriptions from Walldürn (39) scattered picturesquely about the grounds. This is not very scientific, but it is charming. Probably nowhere else is it possible to study Roman ruins in such a park, where buffalo, wild boar, and red deer roam, suitably restrained, against a background of sequoia, linden, spruce, cypress, larch, Douglas fir, and hemlock. Just north of Eulbach, at Hainhaus/Vielbrunn (47) the line of the earthwork of the Domitianic camp can be traced around a simple forest inn.

The anchor-point of the Odenwald Limes is Bad Wimpfen (54-55), where it strikes the Neckar. Here there were two *castella*, now built over, but the medieval wall of Bad

**4.11 Stockstadt, coin hoard**

Wimpfen im Tal is on the footings of the Roman *castellum*, and the Stiftskirche is built over the Roman headquarters building. In Bad Wimpfen am Berg, also, the church stands where the Roman cohort-commander once lived, and the magnificent view of the Neckar and its valley is not only aesthetically satisfying, but also shows how well this post commanded traffic by river and road. It is worth noting, before we leave the Neckar, that Stuttgart, the present capital of Baden-Württemberg, took its origins from the Limes-*castellum* of Cannstatt, now a suburb.

Returning now to the eastern branch of the Limes, the straight stretch built under Antoninus Pius, we can trace almost the whole wall of the unusual *castellum* at Osterburken (40). What is unusual about it is that it has an annex. The usual rectangular fort with rounded corners, visible in the model (Fig. 4.12) is now almost entirely built over, but about A.D. 190 Marcus Aurelius' lamentable son Commodus built the addition, to control the slope that dangerously overlooks the original camp. Skeletons of Alemannic invaders, their hands chopped off, testify to the savagery of the last-ditch defense in A.D. 260. Here, too, the soldiery was devoted to Mithras: nearby was found, in 1861, carefully bedded in sand, a famous relief. It portrays scenes from Mithras' life story, to be described from another example in Chapter 6; it provided important evidence for the Belgian Franz Cumont's pioneering book, *Oriental Religions in Roman Paganism*. The excellent condition of the

**4.12 Osterburken, model**

**4.13 Limes-marker north of Murrhardt, woodcarving**

relief, now on view in the Badisches Landesmuseum in Karlsruhe, is due to a promise of beer to the workmen who excavated it, which inspired them to get it out whole. The excavator of Osterburken was one of the great pioneers of Roman archaeology in Germany, Karl Schumacher. It is pleasant to record that the road leading from the town to the *castellum* is named Prof. Schumacherstrasse.

Of the next *castellum* south, Jagsthausen (41), little remains, but it is worth a visit as a striking illustration of the continuity of history. For over the remains of the Roman fort, where once the headquarters building stood, rises the medieval seat of Götz von Berlichingen of the Iron Hand, one of Germany's great sixteenth-century knights, for a time leader of the Peasant Revolt, and hero of a play by Goethe that is annually presented in the castle courtyard. In the little castle-museum, along with Roman finds, is Götz's iron hand itself, which he wore to replace his own, hacked off in battle. The castle is still in the possession of the von Berlichingen family, and they have turned part of it into a charming inn.

From Jagsthausen south, the line of the Limes earthwork and remains of watch-towers is easily followed, since, by exception, the modern highway parallels it, and is well provided with markers. One, in carved wood in the tradition of old inn signs, amusingly portrays a quizzical Roman soldier and a bearded German facing one another in mild surmise across the Limes (Fig. 4.13).

**113**

4.14 Limes south of Welzheim, air view

At Mainhardt (43) a weatherbeaten signboard gives a plan of the fort, and a small local museum houses the finds. Murrhardt (44), a charming town with a *cordon bleu* hotel (the Sonne-Post) preserves in its Friedenstrasse the line of the Roman road, and the east gate of the *castellum* is distinguished by a marker. South of Welzheim (45) the line of the Limes ditch (Pfahlgraben) is clearly visible from the air (Fig. 4.14), running straight as a die across the fertile fields.

At Lorch (63), where the Raetian Limes begins (map, Fig. 4.15), the north half of the *castellum* lies under the churchyard, and there are Roman stones in the churchyard wall. At Aalen (66), the excellent new Limesmuseum, opened in 1964, lies directly over the largest *castellum* between the Rhine and the Danube (for 1,000 men); the foundations of the camp's main gate lie just outside the museum's front windows. The museum houses a splendid collection of air-photographs of Roman sites along the Danube, invisible to the naked eye on the ground, but showing up in air-photographs taken in raking light in the dry season, when the outlines of buried walls are revealed by the sparser growth of the crops above.

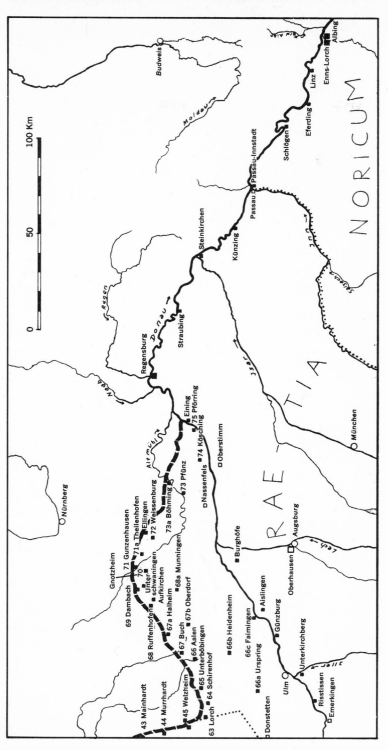

4.15 Map, Raetian Limes

At modern-medieval Weissenburg (72) the *castellum* beyond the railway west of the town narrowly missed discovery in 1884 because the trial trench went straight through the opening of the south gate, striking no remains. But the fort was finally found, and the area has now been made into a park, with the ground-plan restored: the usual double ditch, walls with towers at the rounded corners, and headquarters building with a well in the courtyard. A heated building (the squat piers supporting the floor, creating the empty space through which the warmed air ran, have been restored) must have been the prefect's quarters. There are also barracks and a granary.

Pfünz (73), between six and seven miles behind the Limes, lies on a picturesque height controlling the crossing of the river Altmühl; its name is probably a corruption of the Latin *ad Pontes*, "at the bridges." The bottom courses of its four gates lie in the midst of the waving grain of the fertile fields now tilled above it. In the camp prison the excavators found the leg-bone of a skeleton still in irons; there were Roman wagon wheels in the storehouse. The finding in the fort of the skeletons of an armed watch shows that invaders—probably in A.D. 233—took it by surprise. In the native settlement below, the plans of 137 houses have been plotted, thirteen of them with central heating. They must have been half-timbered and thatched, for no stone or roof tiles were found.

Eining (Abusina), the anchor-point of the walled Limes on the Danube between Ingolstadt and Regensburg, has its walls preserved about a meter high all round, so that its ground-plan is clearly visible: the usual headquarters building, commandant's house, and barracks; outside the wall to the north the remains of a heated house and elaborate baths; earlier baths to the west, overlooking the Abens canal. In the southwest corner a buttressed, bastioned wall, built very late in the fort's history, cuts off a corner seventy feet square for last-ditch defense by a minimum force. The

**116**

fort was built under Vespasian, went through the usual phases, and after A.D. 141 was manned by a detachment of Britons, deliberately displaced after a revolt in their province.

The Raetian Limes proper ends at Eining, but *castella* continue at intervals down the Danube to Regensburg, and on into Austria. Regensburg (Castra Regina) is the fourth city of Roman Raetia—along with Bregenz, Kempten, and Augsburg—and its northernmost outpost. In existence as a 500-man fort since Vespasian's time (after A.D. 74), it was burnt down in the Marcomanni uprising that plagued the reign of Marcus Aurelius, and rebuilt in A.D. 179, as we know from an immense inscription found in 1873 at the main gate of the restored camp, and now in the Regensburg museum. Castra Regina was no mere *castellum* for a 500-man detachment, like the ordinary Limes forts: it measured 1770 x 1476 feet, large enough for a legion; indeed, the inscription just mentioned states that a legion was stationed here. Modern building activity in the rapidly growing city uncovered in 1955 the southeast corner of the *castra*-wall (Fig. 4.16), of squared stone. It belongs to the Limes of Diocletian (*ca.* A.D. 300), but follows the line of Marcus Aurelius' camp, which had four corner towers and eighteen intermediate ones. Of these the most famous flanked the main gate on the north, facing the Danube. It is preserved to a height of thirty-six feet (Fig. 4.17), through having been incorporated into a convent, now the Bischofshof Hotel. Regensburg's civilian settlement was elegant and Romanized enough to have porticoed streets. Near the railroad station, a cemetery, which had to be excavated under emergency conditions, contained 6,000 graves, of which only 1,500 could be recorded. When Stilicho, a Vandal general in Roman service, was forced to recall troops in 401 to fight Alaric in Italy, Regensburg was doomed, but there is some evidence that Roman forces were still there in 430, and references in the eighth century to its beetling walls suggest that Regensburg is one of the Roman sites that may have been continuously occupied into the Middle Ages.

Twenty-five miles down the Danube from Regensburg lies Straubing (Sorviodunum), a *castellum* for two cohorts, with the usual history: Flavian earthwork, Hadrianic reinforcement in wood, Antonine phase in stone, destruction by barbarian hordes in A.D. 233; i.e., by a wave of Alemanni earlier than the major invasion of 260. So far, nothing

**4.16 Regensburg, *castra* wall, southeast corner**

**4.17 Regensburg, Porta Praetoria**

remarkable; but in 1950 workmen digging in the grounds of a Roman villa, possibly the camp commander's, about two miles from the fort, hit upon a large copper basin, lying upside down in the earth only sixteen inches below the surface. In idle curiosity they struck a hole through it with a pick, and to their surprise saw that the basin was crammed with objects in bronze and iron, 115 of them, as it turned out. The workmen cut the hole larger with tinsmiths' shears, and roughly pulled the objects out. Among the iron pieces were a sword, a dagger, a spear point, a saw, a crow-bar, a scythe, a bit, horseshoes, a curry-comb, leg-irons, keys, hooks, a bell, and barrel-hoops, but most important was the bronze parade armor, the most remarkable find of the sort ever made, a treasure rivaling that of Hildesheim. Especially interesting were the greaves (leg-protectors),

**119**

4.18 Straubing treasure, Hellenistic face-mask

face-masks, and protective armor for horses, all in bronze, and all decorated in relief. The face-masks were of two types, Hellenistic (Fig. 4.18) and Near Eastern (Fig. 4.19). The Near Eastern type is particularly striking, with its pointed wig, perhaps intended to represent fleece. It is Syrian work, and the local cohort came from Syria. The excavators think the armor may have been used in tournaments in honor of some Syrian hero whose cult the Syrian troops had brought from home. The face-protector for a horse (Fig. 4.20) is no less interesting, with its embossed Minerva, Victory, and snakes. Unfortunately no account was taken of stratification when the treasure was found, so that the date of its burial is controversial. Since the various pieces, like those of the Hildesheim treasure, belonged to different owners (they have various names scratched on them), and since the style of the reliefs is that of the Severan dynasty (A.D. 193-235), the best hypothesis is that the hoard was put together and hidden by metal-robbers in the crisis of 233.

Thirty miles farther down the Danube from Straubing is Künzing, a 500-man *castellum* where careful work has established three building phases, the latest in stone, probably of before A.D. 132, when the cohort assigned to the fort was withdrawn to Judea for service against the Jewish revolt. The illustration (Fig. 4.21) shows the result of close observation in excavating the southeast corner-tower: an earthwork with wooden battlements and platform in the first phase, perhaps Domitianic; the earthwork changed to a wood-faced wallwalk with a wooden approach-stair in the second phase (Trajanic); and, finally, the battlements and tower replaced with stone, and the sloping earthwork restored, in the third, Hadrianic phase.

Lauriacum (Lorch, near Enns) was referred to incidentally in the last chapter, but is appropriate to discuss here as a slightly atypical Limes *castra*. This was the site of the first battle described by Tolstoy in *War and Peace*. As we

**4.20 Straubing treasure, protective armor for horse**

saw, Lauriacum began under Claudius. But at that time it was an earthwork for a small detachment, perhaps 200 men. It was destroyed in the Marcomannic War of A.D. 166-180, and the legion moved to Albing, on an island in the Danube. But we now know that it was rebuilt in A.D. 205. The evidence is an impressive building-inscription found in re-use as the sill of a late Roman dwelling on the site of the camp shrine. Lauriacum was a full-sized legionary camp, measuring 1,768 x 1,305 feet, or fifty-three acres—bigger than Carnuntum or Vienna. It was also a station for the Danube fleet. What is atypical about it is that its shape is not the canonical rectangle with rounded corners, but a

**4.19 Straubing treasure, Near Eastern face-mask**

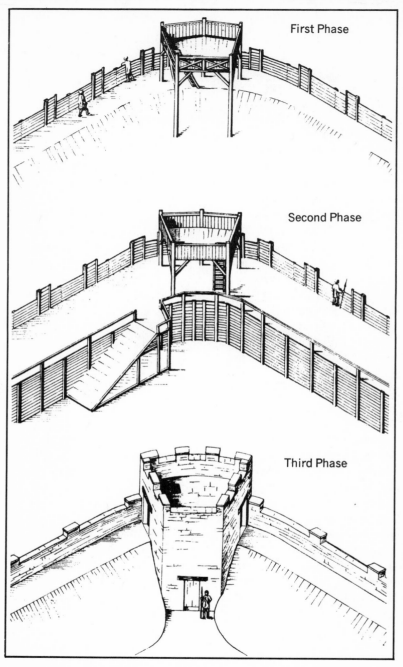

First Phase

Second Phase

Third Phase

4.21 Künzing, corner tower, phases, reconstruction drawing

parallelogram, an instance of adapting military engineering theory to the practical dictates of terrain. The streets of suburban Enns, which overlie the camp, still follow the original Roman diagonals. Besides barracks, the camp had its sick bay, armory, and baths within the walls. The commandant's quarters were unusually tasteful, built around a courtyard with elegant Ionic columns. Adjoining the camp on the west was the civilian settlement, on a grid plan, excavated but now covered over, not like Augst, Köln, or Avenches, but rhomboid, in imitation of the camp. The church of St. Laurenz was built over an altar to the Capitoline triad, the most sacred Christian spot taking over, without breach of continuity, the most sacred Roman one. Fragments of a bronze inscription show that Caracalla gave the settlement municipal rights in the same year (A.D. 212) in which he granted citizenship to the whole Empire. Rich bronzes, including fragments of three life-size statues, show that the town prospered, perhaps from the profits of a shield factory for which there is late evidence.

The Limes had been expensive to build, and even more expensive to maintain. Unless such military security as it afforded resulted in economic prosperity for the area protected, the Empire would not be a viable proposition. So we turn to the archaeological evidence from behind the Limes. Ten of the cities of Germany with over 100,000 population today were Roman foundations: Köln, Frankfurt, Stuttgart, Wiesbaden, Augsburg, Bonn, Mainz, Heidelberg, Regensburg, and Neuss; and, of these, three, Stuttgart, Wiesbaden, and Mainz, are capitals of *Länder*. Obviously the Romans chose their sites well, and it is reasonable to assume that originally the prosperity of these places was protected by the Limes. All of them have been or will be discussed in this book. Frankfurt, for example, proves from postwar excavation in bombed areas around the Cathedral and the marketplace to have started as a Domitianic *castellum* (the evidence for date is pottery), and the market was a commercial center from the beginning.

The area which includes the Black Forest, the Neckar valley, and the Swabian Alb was known to the Romans as the *Agri Decumates*, a term whose meaning is controversial: perhaps "Land of the Ten Cantons." Vespasian first opened up this territory with his road from Strassburg to the Danube in A.D. 73 or 74, and his son Domitian must have meant to enhance its prosperity when he organized the permanent defense of the Limes on its eastern frontier after A.D. 90. Some of the evidence for prosperity, in the rich villas (over 800 are known) and affluent spas like Baden-Baden and Badenweiler, will be discussed in the next chapter, along with Wiesbaden and others. We must also mention in passing that the storied university city of Heidelberg takes its origin from a pair of Roman camps— hardly more than police posts—in what is now the suburb of Neuenheim across the Neckar, at the junction of five or six Roman roads. A wooden bridge connected the main camp with the civilian settlement across the river. The district was sufficiently pacified by A.D. 125 for the troops to be moved, perhaps forward to the Limes. The civilian settlement on the south bank survived, and modern Heidelberg overlies it.

More important than Heidelberg in antiquity was Lopodunum (nowadays Ladenburg: present population 7,000, compared to Heidelberg's 126,000), the anchor-point on the Neckar of a trunk highway leading north up the east bank of the Rhine to Kastel (for Mainz) and Wiesbaden (Aquae Mattiacorum). Lopodunum began as a Claudian earthwork fort. Domitian rebuilt it in stone, but the Limes apparently made its garrison unnecessary, for in A.D. 116 Trajan transferred its troops to Pannonia. The civil settlement survived as Civitas Ulpia Sueborum Nicretum. (Ulpia was Trajan's family name, and the Nicretes were one of the ten cantons of the *Agri Decumates*.) The excavated phase of the town was planned, a century after Trajan, as a small imitation of Trajan's Rome. The basilica ran across the end of the forum, as there.* It was unfinished. When its building began, in the early third century A.D., the Limes was no longer guaranteeing either security or prosperity. Over the basilica was built the church of St. Gallus. We have seen churches rise from pagan temples and from military shrines: in both cases there is religious continuity. But when a church rose over a basilica, a secular building, the continuity was not one of religious significance but of secular pomp, for the Roman basilica, with its broad nave, columns, and two side aisles, was often the most impressive building in a Roman town.

As a final example of civilian prosperity protected by the Limes, we may take Arae Flaviae, nowadays Rottweil, where the Roman road from Vindonissa to Augsburg crossed the Neckar south of Rottenburg. (Rottenburg, which in antiquity bore the Celtic name Sumelocenna, was itself an important center from Flavian times onward.) Arae Flaviae, originally a *castellum*, was abandoned as a military post in Flavian times: again the Limes provided sufficient protection so that it could develop as a civilian town. Its name, "Flavian Altars," suggests that Vespasian was imitating Augustus. It was designed, like Köln, the Ara Ubiorum, to concentrate native loyalty around the Imperial cult. Its identity, its self-governing status as a *municipium*, and its survival at least down into Antonine times are guaranteed by the find of a wooden writing tablet dated A.D. 186, recording the punishment of Germans for besieging Strassburg. A late-second-century mosaic of the legend-

---

* See *The Mute Stones Speak*, p. 266; paperback, p. 261 (Trajan's Forum, Rome).

ary singer Orpheus charming animals with his music hints at its prosperity, and its yearning toward Graeco-Roman culture.

It is well to end this predominantly military chapter on a civilian note, for civilian prosperity is what the Limes was designed to guarantee. Not for any predominantly humanitarian or welfare-state reasons: prosperity meant higher tax revenue, without which the Empire could not survive. That the taxes were far from ruinous is proved by the rich villas and the elegant spas which it will be the business of the next chapter to describe.

# 5 : The Good Life

So far, our emphasis has been very heavily military. In this chapter, an attempt will be made to redress the balance, and to describe the blessings enjoyed by civilians under the Roman peace, especially in spas and luxury villas.

Where the Roman won, he built, and where he built, he bathed. The several German sites with hot springs naturally appealed to the Roman sense of practicality, since they saved the expense of heating. Roman doctors recommended the therapeutic qualities of the mineral waters of the hot springs, and the vogue of the spa was born. It began in Germany in the 70s A.D.

In the grounds of the modern spa at Badenweiler, in the Black Forest in southwest Baden-Württemberg (see map, Fig. 5.1), is one of the best-preserved Roman monuments in Germany. It is a pity it is open to the public only on Sundays, and on Tuesdays at 5 P.M. The grounds in which it stands are still in use as a spa, and motor traffic is forbidden, to spare the sensibilities of the clients. It must have appealed to the Romans as a bit of Italy in the raw German land. It is one of the warmest places in Germany: palm, cypress, and banana trees grow there, the wine is famous, and in antiquity there were olives as well. Its history began when Vespasian opened up the *Agri Decumates* about A.D. 74, but it flourished most in the palmy days of the mid-second century. It is of interest as the first scientific excavation on German soil: it was discovered in clearing

**129**

6°   8°   10°

Blankenheim •

Rhine R.

Wittlich
Otrang •   • Wiesbaden
Welschbillig •

50°

Trier •

Igel •   • Nennig

Main R.

Mosel R.

• Baden-Baden

48°

Danube R.

• Badenweiler

Munzach •

Ober-Entfelden •

• Bosceaz

0          50
Miles

46°

stone for the Margrave's quarters in 1784. The model (Fig. 5.2) gives the best idea of the plan; an unsightly but protective roof now prevents an overall view. Originally the baths had a vaulted roof, and glass windows (the excavators found segments of vault, mullions, and broken glass), but neither the rooms nor the water were artificially heated: probably the spa was planned for summer use only. The natural temperature of the water is seventy-eight degrees. At the left of the model is the vestibule. The stepped apsidal pools were originally a pair of dressing rooms. The two square pools have tubs on either side of them for the use of invalids or children. There is another vestibule at the far end. Since things here seem to come in pairs, it has been conjectured that one end of the baths was for soldiers, the other for civilians; or that the sexes were segregated; but the plan may simply reflect the architect's aesthetic sense of balance. In front of the square pools are round ones for a cold plunge, and next to them a pair of steam rooms, with a shrine between, for the baths were dedicated to Diana, who under the native cult-title of Abnoba was the tutelary spirit of the Black Forest. In the rooms in the foreground, clients drank the waters; there were latrines below.

The hot springs of Wiesbaden (Aquae Mattiacorum) were known personally to the elder Pliny, who had served in Germany, and who mentions them in his *Natural History* (A.D. 77). Here, as at the Saalburg, the Roman *castellum* received the not unmixed blessing of restoration at the orders of Kaiser Wilhelm II, but the baths were untouched, for they were—and are—still elegantly in use. There were individual tubs, filled from bronze faucets. Shallow footbaths surround the tubs, to discourage getting in with dirty feet. An epigram of Martial records that the waters were also good for bleaching the hair. Diana was

5.1 Map, spas and villas

5.2 Badenweiler, baths, model

the presiding deity here also: an inscription dedicated by
the wife of the commander of the legion stationed here
gives thanks to the goddess for curing her daughter. The
spa continued to flourish after the troops were withdrawn
from the *castellum* in A.D. 121 or 122. Exercise-grounds
adjoined, where clients worked out anointed with oil (the
containers, clay, glass, or bronze, were found), and after-
wards scraped themselves with a curved instrument called
a strigil, examples of which are on display in the Wiesbaden
museum. Finds of dice show that they found other, less
athletic ways of spending their leisure while taking the cure.

Badenweiler nowadays is comfortably bourgeois, Wiesbaden is elegant, but Baden-Baden, in the Black Forest
between Karlsruhe and Strassburg, is the most elegant of
all. It became in the nineteenth century the favorite resort
of the crowned heads of Europe. We can imagine the
gleaming carriages rolling along the Lichtentaler Allee, the
ladies in crinolines, carrying parasols, and the gentlemen in
top hats. Napoleon III and his Empress, Eugénie, made it
fashionable (the official language was French); Queen Vic-
toria took the cure, and her scapegrace son Edward—later
Edward VII—created a small scandal by riding along the
fashionable promenade dressed in a sheet on his way to a
ghost party. The tradition is one of conspicuous consump-
tion and conspicuous waste: to this day roulette on gala
occasions is played with gold chips.

The tradition of royal patronage at Baden-Baden goes back to Roman times. The Emperor Vespasian built the first baths, and they were much visited, especially from nearby Strassburg. But it was Caracalla (reigned A.D. 211-217), an Imperial rascal who puts Edward VII completely in the shade, who first made the resort fashionable. He visited it in 213, seeking a cure for his arthritis. A building-inscription records his grateful benefactions. He sheared away a cliff, built a bath-building (plan, Fig. 5.3 A-D), which excavation in 1847 proved to be very like the one at Badenweiler, restored the warm baths and refaced them with a veneer of white marble and green granite, and graciously permitted the place to call itself after him, Civitas Aurelia Aquensis. (The upstart Severan dynasty to which Caracalla belonged took the more prestigious family name of Marcus Aurelius.) Inscriptions show that Diana Abnoba was the bath-goddess here, as elsewhere, but Caracalla professed special gratitude to Apollo Grannus, a Celtic water-god adopted into the Roman pantheon.

As the vogue of Baden-Baden increased in the nineteenth

**5.3 Baden-Baden, baths, plan**

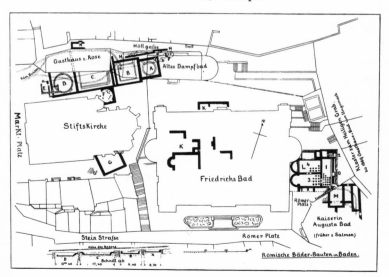

5.4 Baden-Baden, Soldiers' Baths

century, excavation for new bath-buildings revealed more Roman installations; for example, under the Friedrichs Bad, built between 1869 and 1877 (plan, K), and under the Kaiserin Augusta Bad, built 1890-1893 (plan, L,M). The latter rooms (Fig. 5.4), called, on no evidence, the Soldiers' Baths, are roofed and electrically lighted, and open to visitors. They are particularly noteworthy for their elaborate radiant heating, installed to keep the rooms warm in winter, even though the water temperature ranged from 115° to 150°. The subject of radiant heating has been mentioned in passing before; this is a convenient place to discuss it in a little more detail. About 100 B.C. in Italy, C. Sergius Orata ("Orata" means "Goldfish") first used pools heated from below for his fish and oysters. The usage was soon extended, first to baths, then to houses. A luxury in sunny Italy, central heating was almost a necessity in Germany. Heat from wood or charcoal fires in a furnace room passed under and heated a waterproof cement floor suspended on squat brick columns. The cement expanded or contracted under variations of heat and cold without cracking. The walls, built of hollow tiles, could also be heated, to prevent damage to frescoes from humidity. Caracalla's baths at Baden-Baden, with their elaborate engineering and décor, lasted only twenty years, till the Alemanni invaded in A.D.

233. The evidence is a coin hoard found in 1824 in nearby Quettig, containing one gold coin of Galba and 561 silver pieces, of which the latest were minted before the end of the reign of Alexander Severus, who was murdered, as we saw, in Mainz in A.D. 235.

In the security guaranteed by the Limes, villas sprang up like mushrooms. They combined the luxury of mosaics, frescoes, central heating, glazed windows, formal gardens, statuary, pools, fountains, and colonnades with the practicality of a working farm estate. We shall be discussing a selected few in Switzerland, Austria, and the Mosel valley. They conform closely to the norms laid down in the first century B.C. in Rome by Varro; that is, the Italian villa was adapted to German conditions. We have already seen this done at Köln-Müngersdorf.

Varro recommends a sunny, well-watered site exposed to healthful winds, an elevated pasture land at the foot of a wooded hill. The estate should be near a highway, and not too far from a town, where produce may be sold and supplies and services purchased. (A large landowner may find it more economical to have his own service personnel: smiths, doctors, dry cleaners.) A site too close to a swamp or river should be avoided, for fear of mosquitoes. (This advice was ignored by the nabobs who built by the Mosel, where the insect plague in antiquity was apparently not so great as in Italy.) To guard against brigands, the estate should be enclosed, with a hedge, fence, earthwork, or wall. A plantation of elms makes an especially good boundary: vines may be trained on the trunks, the leaves make excellent fodder, and the timber will provide fence-rails and firewood. The working buildings of the farm should be carefully planned: the overseer should have quarters near the entrance, to keep an eye on the coming and going of the farm hands, for whom shacks should be provided. The stables should be in a warm, sheltered place. Barns should have damp-proof floors. There should be sheds for carts and tools, and to protect the newly threshed grain from rain. The wine-press floor should be sloped for drainage. There should be two farmyards. One may be both ornamental and useful, with a columned pool where geese may swim and livestock be watered; the other should contain the straw pile, and compost and manure heaps. Archaeologists have found some or all of these features in the villas about to be described.

The troops at Augst and Vindonissa early began to provide in Switzerland the security in which villas might thrive. One of the most impressive is at Ober-Entfelden, a walled estate covering a couple of square miles, fifteen miles southwest of Vindonissa. Here, as often, large numbers of roof tiles in the fields betrayed the existence of ancient remains. Even the Swiss have unemployment: the unemployed excavated the farm buildings here between 1936 and 1938; the main villa was excavated in the more prosperous early fifties, under a plastic roof for protection against rain. The earliest phase proved to date from the first century A.D.; the villa (Fig. 5.5) was at its most flourishing in the second century; the Alemanni burned the farm buildings in the third. The farmyard was walled, as Varro recommends: it covered 525 x 1,150 feet, or fifteen acres. Built at regular—even regimented—intervals against the enclosure wall were one-room shacks, each with a hearth, for the hired hands. There was a corral big enough for sixty animals. The villa was heated, had baths, and a pleasant terrace on the valley side, but no mosaics. Its outside walls were plastered and painted red, and it rose twenty-six feet above ground level. Unlike the farm buildings, it was not burned, but since there were few small finds, it must have been either sacked or abandoned. A few coins of the fourth century were found in the farmyard, but no late pottery: this suggests late but scanty and impoverished habitation.

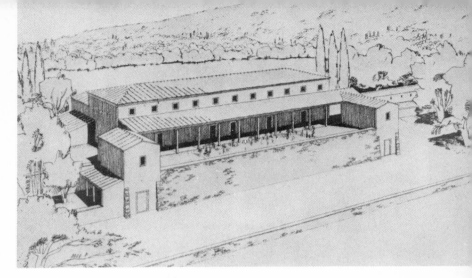

5.5 Ober-Entfelden, villa, model

Ten miles south of Augst, Munatius Plancus' colony, lies the villa of Munzach, named for Plancus (Munzach, corrupted from Monciacum, which was corrupted from Munatiatum). To know the ancient name of a villa is rare; it is rarer still to know the names of the owners. At Munzach we do: they were C. Indutius (a Celtic name) Sallustianus and his wife Victorinia. Their names are on an inscription built into the façade of the local church. The use of praenomen, nomen, and cognomen shows that this local worthy was a Roman citizen. Here, as at Köln-Müngersdorf and probably many other places, natives have prospered, and assimilated Roman ways. This was a working villa, with workrooms attached. Its plan (Fig. 5.6), without corner-towers, was one in vogue about the middle of the first century A.D. Like Ober-Entfelden, the villa prospered most in the second century. The evidence is the hypocaust heating, the baths, a number of mosaics, walls veneered in colored marble, well-stocked cellars, oystershells (proof of gourmet tastes and pocketbook), a fountain, and a bronze table service. The heating system is so well-preserved that we can see the paving details: directly above the squat columns of the hypocaust area, a capstone of tile; above that, a stone pavement; above that, a waterproof level of

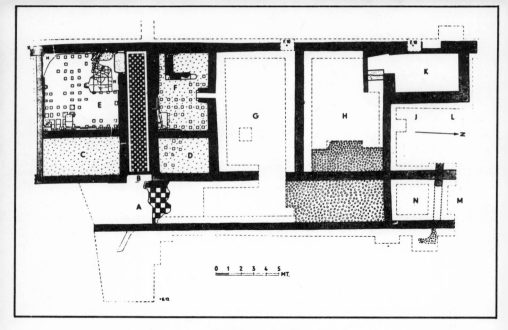

5.6 Munzach, villa, plan

crushed tile mixed with lime; then two layers of mosaic. This is very close to the method laid down by the Augustan architect Vitruvius in his standard work *De Architectura*. The mosaics are fragmentary, but we can see a peacock in one, a four-horse chariot in another, and it is also clear that they lasted long enough to need patching. Then a catastrophe: the Alemannic invasion of 260, indicated by a burnt level, after which the house was again lived in, but the heating system no longer worked.

A mosaic is the chief surviving feature of a villa with farm buildings at Boscéaz, near Orbe, twenty miles north of Lausanne and eight miles southwest of Yverdon, at the end of Lake Neuchâtel. Here the dating is from coins: the earliest, of Nero (A.D. 54-68) or Domitian (81-96); the latest, of Gratian (A.D. 367-383). It is fortunate that visitors now are more welcome than they were in 1846, when the local farmer, exasperated at crowds of tourists trampling his crops, took a pickax to one of the mosaics. The motifs are various: a labyrinth surrounded by a wall with gates and

138

towers; the days of the week beginning with Saturday, represented by gods (Saturn, Sol, Luna, Mars, Mercury, Jupiter, Venus) in medallions, plus Ganymede being carried off by Jupiter disguised as an eagle, and Narcissus admiring himself in a mirror. The whole is framed by a series of wild animals being chased by dogs (one on a leash). The one illustrated (Fig. 5.7) shows a loaded four-wheeled wagon drawn by a yoke of oxen driven by a man with a goad; then a controversial central figure; then a man with a horn and club. The interpretation of the mosaic depends upon the explanation of the central figure. He may be a fisherman, with bucket and pole, or a fowler with a bucket of birdlime and a bundle of sticks, or may be carrying torches and a brazier. Some scholars give up, and see no connection among the three scenes, but most interpret them as a hunting triptych: the oxcart is loaded with hunting nets, to spread in the unsportsmanlike Roman fashion across the trail to the animals' water hole, and the other two figures are beaters, the horn a hunting horn. The animals being hunted around the edge of the mosaic already described provide an argument in favor of the hunting interpretation: the lord of this manor will have been a hunting, shooting, fishing type.

**5.7 Boscéaz, mosaic**

The provinces of Noricum (Austria) and Pannonia (Hungary) were also pleasantly dotted with villas. At Katsch (ancient Chatissa) in Upper Styria, on a terrace with a mountain view above the river Mur, quarrying operations in the late twenties revealed the ground-plan (Fig. 5.8) of a modest but pleasant farmhouse with painted, not marble-veneered walls, and no mosaics. Enough remained to permit a reconstruction (Fig. 5.9). Room 1 was a vestibule, with its arched entrance and pediment; 2–6 were living quarters, of which 6 was heated, and 5 a porch; 18 a veranda, and 19 a courtyard; the rest were workrooms. There were farm buildings adjacent, and also a cemetery, with both cremation and inhumation burials, and pottery datable between 50 and 150 A.D. Nothing in this attractive farmstead is dated later than A.D. 166, when it was destroyed by fire. It was a casualty of the Marcomannic War, which

**5.8 Katsch, villa, plan**

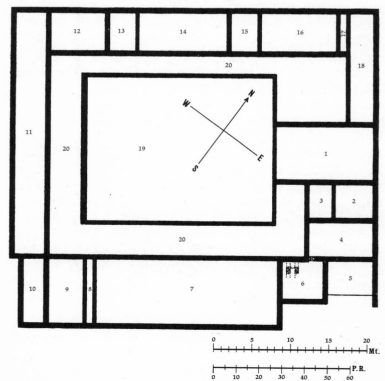

**5.9  Katsch, villa, reconstruction drawing**

brought tribulation not only to Marcus Aurelius, but also to his subjects, like those who suffered tragic loss of life and property here.

The richest villa of the hundred known in Pannonia is Parndorf, between the Neusiedler See and the Danube, about ten miles south of Carnuntum, which must have been its market town. The estate wall encloses thirty acres, dotted with farm buildings, including a porter's lodge, a heated cottage for one of the hired hands and his family, baths, and a granary. The main villa (Fig. 5.10) has its outer walls painted in squares, to imitate cut stone. The squares are splotched with white, yellow, red, and black. The inner walls show equally clashing colors, sometimes imitating marble, in a style that can only be described as Early Men's Room; taste is not the strong point here. The villa had thirty-four rooms, all heated, and at least eleven with mosaic floors. Some mosaics are geometric, others figured: Dionysus, Diana, Bellerophon (who rode Pegasus, the winged horse) slaying the monstrous Chimaera, part lion, part goat, part serpent. The painted walls are painful to describe: red and blue rosettes on an ocher ground; yellow and dark-green squares outlined in red and black; green, red, and yellow leaves, with yellow, blue and black splotches, against a white background; a yellow, red, and gray field dotted with small white triangles; red lozenges outlined in white

**141**

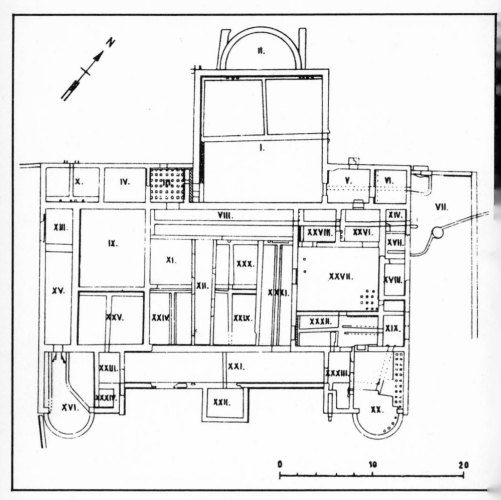

5.10 Parndorf, villa, plan

on a blue-green and yellow field. Rooms XIV and XXVI
must have been nurseries: on the walls are childish sketches
of horses and riders, and a woman in a long dress, labeled
Quirina, leading by the hand a child carrying a fruit basket,
and labeled Petronia. The earliest phase of this extraordinarily tasteless phantasmagoria is dated about A.D. 100,
with a rebuilding about 300, to which the apsidal rooms and
the mosaics belong.

The richest villa area in Germany lies in and north of the Mosel valley, in the northern part of the modern *Land* of Rheinland-Pfalz. Here, in the Eifel massif at Blankenheim, thirty miles southwest of Bonn, just off the Roman military road from Köln to Trier, careful excavation in 1894 and 1914 made possible the restoration, in a model, of two phases (Figs. 5.11 and 5.12) of a villa less pretentious than Parndorf, as comfortable as Katsch. It lasted, on the evidence of pottery and coins, from before A.D. 100 to about 350. It faced east, overlooking the lovely Ahr valley, where the Burgundy-like German red wine is grown. On either side of it, eastward, were the farm buildings, in an enclosed area measuring 800 x 400 feet. The excavators found that gray, sandy, lime-poor mortar identified the earliest phase of the main villa, which had twenty rooms, with corridors and cellar, baths in the northwest corner (photograph, right), projecting wings joined by a hundred-foot veranda with a view, and a roof of thin stone slabs like slates. This phase lasted till about A.D. 150, when the villa was destroyed by fire. The final phase (third to mid-fourth century) is identified by the use of red mortar. Its outer walls were stuccoed red. The projecting wings were abolished, and the veranda extended to double its original length (Fig. 5.12). The entrance was now on the south (around the corner of the veranda to the left), more rooms were heated, the number of rooms nearly doubled (sometimes by running cross-walls across existing rooms), and a furnace room was added to the baths (low shed-like projection, photograph, right). The latrine was ingeniously flushed by the run-off water from the adjoining baths, which had an altar to Fortune in their vestibule, and a semicircular pool four and a half to five feet deep. The end of this phase shows a decline: the heating system fell out of use, and the south end was abandoned as a habitation and used for storage. A coin of the Emperor Magnentius dates the final phase from A.D. 350 to 353.

5.11 Blankenheim, villa, first phase, model

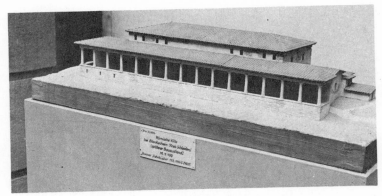

5.12 Blankenheim, villa, third phase, model

The heartland of the German villa region is farther south, in the Mosel valley itself. We are fortunate that the Mosel, that charming, vine-girt stream, has its late Latin poet, Ausonius. Professor, provincial governor, consul, he lived for a while, a little before A.D. 375, at Trier, which at that time was one of the four capitals of the Roman Empire. We shall be returning in the last chapter to Trier, the most impressive of all Roman cities in Germany. Ausonius was there as tutor to the future Emperor Gratian. He was moved to describe, in 483 hexameter lines, the beauties of his temporary home. His poem begins where the Mosel meets the Rhine; he waxes lyrical, in epic meter, about the crystal waters, the fish and the fishing, the vintners, the vineyards reflected in the pellucid stream, the mock naval battles, and the villas, in many of which, as a member of the Establishment, he must have been a welcome guest.

The most impressive of all the Mosel villas is at Otrang, just off the main Trier-Köln highway northeast of Bitburg, which is twenty miles north of Trier. It stands on a terrace bounded by an estate wall measuring 1,250 x 443 feet, or thirty-six acres. So palatial an estate must have belonged to the Imperial fisc; it was probably a stud farm. It has been calculated that it would cost three to four million dollars to build today. The outer walls were weatherproofed red-brown; the roof was red tile. There are no less than sixty-six rooms (Fig. 5.13), of which fifteen have mosaics, all of geometric pattern, none of them with figures. Geometric mosaics were in fashion about A.D. 100; the villa was in its prime about fifty years later. It faced west, but there was also a sunny veranda with a southern exposure (see model, Fig. 5.14). There were two sets of baths (rooms 3-13 and 24-29; room 14 was a latrine). Rooms 17-23 were the living quarters of the first phase, rooms 43-46 and 63-66 of the second; room 46 was for open-air dining. Apsidal porches (1, 19, 61, 66) afforded views in three directions, north, south and east; westward lay the farm buildings. The wine cellars, for the exquisite white wine of the country, lay under rooms 61, 62, and 66. The villa was in part two-storied: 32 and 37 are stairwells. The whole effect is one of restrained elegance, much more tasteful than Parndorf.

At Wittlich on the Lieser, eleven miles northwest of Bernkastel, where the finest Mosel wine of all is bottled, are the remains of a particularly attractive villa directly on the water (see reconstruction-drawing, Fig. 5.15). There were villas very much like it on the shores of the Bay of Naples. A fresco representing one of them, nearly a twin to Wittlich, is in the National Museum in Naples: it comes from the House of Lucretius Fronto in Pompeii. At Witt-

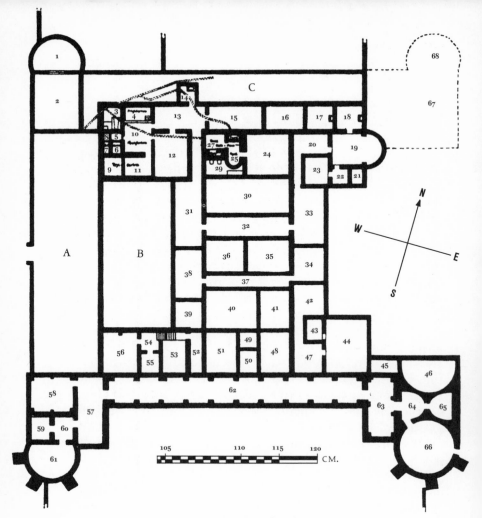

5.13 Otrang, villa, plan

5.14 Otrang, villa, model

5.15 Wittlich, villa, reconstruction drawing

lich a two-storied arcade facing the river, with a central hall behind, connected the bath-block with the living quarters. These luxury villas, with their wide, fine views, sunny, light rooms, and long vistas of wings, galleries, terraces, and formal gardens, must have been pleasant to live in. They testify to the prosperity, in the second century A.D., of the wine trade, or other trades that we shall be investigating, on archaeological evidence, in later chapters.

The villa at Nennig, in the Saarland near the Luxemburg border, on the Mosel twenty-five miles southwest of Trier, equals Otrang in elegance, though not in extent. The villa, painted Pompeian red, was planned primarily for summer use, since its long, shady veranda faces northwest (see plan, Fig. 5.16,1), but the southern suite of rooms in the main block has a southern exposure, for winter use. The core of the plan is the central room, with the aesthetically perfect dimensions of the Golden Section, where one side is related to the other in the proportion .618:1.oo. The room contains an almost perfectly preserved mosaic depicting scenes from the gladiatorial arena, to be described

**147**

below. North of it, facing a court with a fountain, is a suite of rooms for summer living; west of them are the work-rooms. The living rooms were frescoed: mounted Amazons, wild beasts, plants, geometric patterns. A service tunnel, or cryptoporticus, runs around the sides and back of the main

5.16 Nennig, villa and grounds, plan

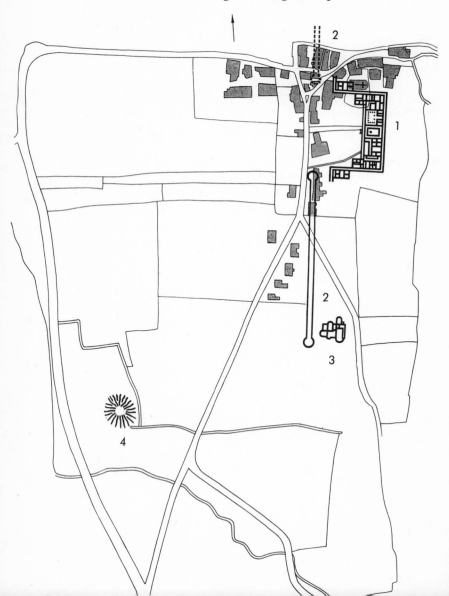

villa rectangle. Beyond each wing were temple-like wings, used as guest houses.

From the southern guest house there runs for 836 feet a covered walkway (plan, 2) decorated with statuary. It gave protected access to the baths (3), which are of record size: about 100 feet square, larger in themselves than most American middle-class houses. They were equipped with all modern conveniences: a pool measuring 700 square feet, seven bathing rooms, five of them apsidal, and three of them heated. Southwest of the baths was the family mausoleum (plan, 4) nowadays called the Mahlknopf, which is nearly as impressive as those of Augustus and Hadrian (the Castel Sant' Angelo) in Rome.*

A brook meandered through the sloping garden behind: the villa lies on the slope of a hill, as Varro recommends. The brook fed the fountains in the garden, and watered the trees, and the shrubs and hedges clipped in all the fantasies of the topiary art. There were terraces, grottoes, and sculpture, anticipating the formal designs of Italian Renaissance architects, who were inspired by Roman originals.

The mosaic in the central room of the villa has been hailed as the greatest artistic creation of its kind north of the Alps. There are six octagonal medallions and one square; the base of a fountain occupies another large octagonal space. The scenes of gladiatorial combat must be imagined as taking place in the amphitheater at Trier. They are mostly sanguinary: Romans in Italy had as great a taste for blood sports as the modern *aficionado* of football, boxing, or bullfighting, and they passed their taste on unabated to the provinces. In the Nennig mosaic, a tigress mauls a copiously bleeding wild ass; a full-fed lion, with its paw on a wild ass' head, is pulled off by a slave, whose pluck we must admire more than his judgment. A spearsman, having

* See *The Mute Stones Speak*, pp. 154-156; 292-294; paperback, 149-153; 289-290, 292.

mortally wounded a panther (we see the poor beast vainly trying to pull a broken spear from its side) raises his hand in an appeal for applause. There is a fight between gladiators, one armed with a quarterstaff, the other with a whip. A gladiator with a trident fights another in full armor; the referee stands between. A bear (Fig. 5.17) mauls a prostrate gladiator, while two others fight him off with whips. As a counterbalance to these scenes of violence, we are offered an illustration of the musical accompaniment to the games. One musician plays a horn that curves over his shoulder, the other a water-organ, the mechanism of which will be described in Chapter 7 (Figs. 7.16 and 7.17). As the proprietor of Boscéaz spent his leisure in hunting, so the master of Nennig spent his at the arena. If they had had more social conscience, the decline and fall of the Roman Empire might perhaps have been postponed, and we should have been the poorer by two mosaics.

This consideration brings us to the question of the date of Nennig. When the mosaic was taken up for repairs in 1960, a coin of Commodus was found under the floor. Commodus, Marcus Aurelius' villainous son, who fancied himself as a gladiator, reigned from A.D. 180 to 192. With the coin were found fragments of mortar, terracotta, and painted stucco from an earlier phase of the villa.

The question of the date was complicated in 1866 by its excavator's announcement that he had discovered a series of frescoes portraying the Emperor Trajan (reigned A.D. 98-117), and an inscription recording Trajan's presenting the villa to the Secundini, a family of prosperous merchants whose grave-monument at Igel, on the Mosel five miles southwest of Trier, will be described in the last chapter. This coincidence seemed—and in fact was—too good to be true. It transpired that the excavator had forged the inscription, and sent a notice of its discovery to the papers twenty-four hours *before* the planted forgery was actually "found." Also, he had forged the frescoes, anticipating the

5.17 Nennig, mosaic, gladiators and bear

ingenuity of Hollywood by aging them with soot. The great German Roman historian Theodor Mommsen, asked for advice, recommended calling the police, and there was thus spread upon the record the most notorious forgery in the annals of Roman archaeology in Germany.

Finally, we turn to the villa at Welschbillig, halfway between Otrang and Trier. Its most remarkable feature was a pool (Fig. 5.18) 190 feet long and 60 feet wide, big and deep enough to stage the mock naval battles mentioned by Ausonius. It was bordered by 112 busts (herms) of famous Greeks, barbarians, and Romans. Sixty-nine of these were excavated in good condition in 1891-2 and sent to the Landesmuseum in Trier. One of them has been romantically identified as representing Ausonius himself. The villa was certainly in existence in his time, for it was rebuilt after the barbarian invasion of A.D. 260.

5.18 Welschbillig villa, pool with herms, reconstruction drawing

The Welschbillig villa lies in the southern part of an enormous walled estate with a perimeter of over forty-three miles, enclosing a 132-square-mile area. Folklore once charmingly explained the wall as the support for a wine pipeline, designed to feed into the Köln aqueduct. The almost equally charming notion that the enclosed area was a huge cageless zoo for bears must regretfully be rejected, on the ground that the terrain, which is thickly forested parkland, is unsuitable for bears, though it is an appropriate habitat for deer and smaller game. What it was in fact was an Imperial domain, transformed in the very late Empire (fourth or fifth century A.D.) into a hunting preserve or stud farm. Much of what was visible of the wall as late as 1840 has now been destroyed by road-building and stone-robbing. What remains is so crudely built that it could not be the work of professional masons, and indeed

surviving building-inscriptions state that soldiers built it, in
500-foot stretches. In the second and third centuries A.D.
there were over 1,000 settlements in the area, not counting
the numerous limekilns. In the less prosperous days of the
fourth century, the number of settlements was reduced to
forty. Large numbers of slag heaps are evidence that mining
went on here, and there was much quarrying of sandstone
and limestone for the buildings of Trier. It would also,
like Otrang nearby, have served admirably as a stud farm.
The horses of this region—the Eifel—have always been
famous for their endurance; Napoleon, for example, preferred them to all others. The horse-goddess Epona was
worshiped in the area, and the symbol of Trier is a mounted
Amazon—one of the fresco motifs, we may recall, of the
Nennig villa. There was need for a constant supply of
horses for racing in the circus at Trier, and the soldiers who
built the estate wall may have been cavalry, in constant
need of remounts. The well-watered parkland, with its firm
limestone substructure, would have been ideal for horse
rearing. And so the vast estate of which the Welschbillig
villa forms a small part gives evidence of active economic
life, and even of surplus for luxury, as late as the fifth
century A.D.: the presence of the Imperial court at Trier
kept the area prosperous long after the cities and country-
side farther east had lapsed into the doldrums of the Dark
Ages.

This chapter has dealt largely with the worship of
Mammon. It will be appropriate in the next chapter to
discuss the archaeological evidence for the worship of gods
in Roman Germany: the vogue of Near Eastern deities, and
the curious adaptation of Roman to native religion, and
vice versa, which proves the extent, and the limits, of
Romanization.

# 6 : Other Gods
# Than Ours

Wᴇ know most about religion in Roman
Germany from the second to the fifth centuries ᴀ.ᴅ. The
archaeological picture is not simple, because the influences
on belief were complex. To begin with, the Romans viewed
their own official religion (Olympian gods, deified Emperors) with the slightly bored tolerance of most members
of the British Establishment toward the Anglican Church.
There was little or no missionary zeal: provincials were free
to worship whatever gods they pleased, as long as they
paid lip service to the deified Emperors, and were not sub-
versive. The deification of Emperors itself was a political
policy, not a religious act. The alleged apotheosis of a mad-
man like Caligula simply shows how irreligious the Roman
ruling class really was. The core of the Roman state religion
was, consequently, found in the camps; we have seen how
each had a shrine for the worship of the military standards
and the Emperor's statue. In no major city of Roman
Germany is a major temple to the gods of the official religion preserved: the scanty remains under St. Maria im
Kapitol in Köln are the exception that proves the rule.

It is reported of Josef Stalin in World War II that, when
told that the Pope would not like one of his proposed
courses of action, he replied, "The Pope? The Pope? How

6.1 Map for Chapters 6–8

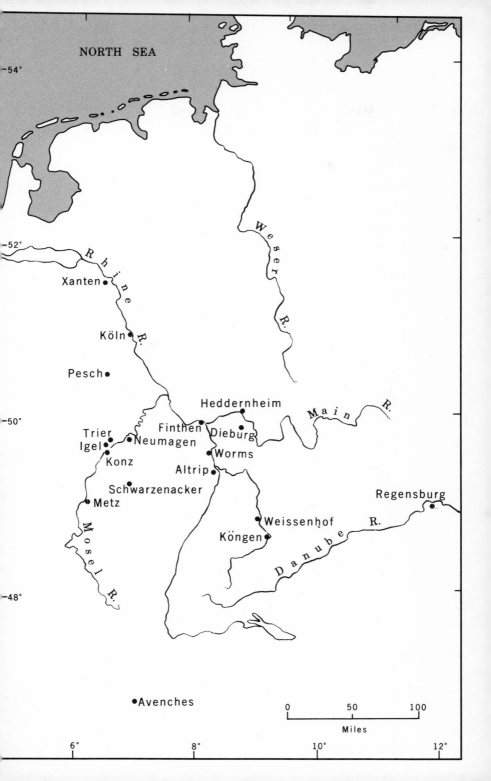

NORTH SEA

−54°

−52°

Xanten

Köln

Pesch

Heddernheim

Trier
Igel
Konz
Neumagen
Finthen
Dieburg
Worms
Altrip

Schwarzenacker

Metz

Weissenhof
Köngen

Regensburg

Rhine R.

Weser R.

Main R.

Danube R.

Mosel R.

−50°

−48°

Avenches

0    50    100
Miles

6°        8°        10°        12°

many divisions has *he* got?" Roman "tolerance" of native religion was of the Stalin sort: the Romans, like him, simply did not think religion was important. The result, as archaeology reveals it in Germany, was a very wide variety of cults. In the area of Roman occupation, evidence of pure Teutonic cult is rare; Celtic gods had many more votaries. And because so many soldiers, and so many camp followers selling goods to the soldiers, came from the Near East, Near Eastern cults had a very wide following in Roman Germany; among the Near Eastern cults was Christianity.

The data of this chapter can best be reduced to order by treating first a selection from the archaeological evidence for the official Roman religion, and thereafter German, Celtic, and Near Eastern cults, concluding with Christianity.

Because large cities, surviving and prospering in our own times, tend to wipe out their own past, the best archaeological evidence for Roman cult in Germany comes from places as obscure now as in antiquity. One of these is Schwarzenacker, near Einöd (Saarland: see map, Fig. 6.1). It was a station on the Roman road between Metz (Divodurum) and Worms (Borbetomagus). The village was burned in the Alemannic invasion of 260, and a collection of bronze statuettes from Italy, of religious import, fell through the floor of a frescoed room in one of the houses, and was found in the cellar. The earliest statuette (Fig. 6.2), dated on stylistic grounds A.D. 20-40, is of a young, beardless male figure identified as the Genius of the Roman People. To the Romans, a Genius was an attendant spirit or guardian angel, a personification. That of the Roman Senate was represented as a bearded, mature figure; that of the Roman People was younger, and beardless. (It will be noted that this abstraction is at least as much political as religious.) The Schwarzenacker Genius holds in his right hand a knobbed scepter, in his left originally a horn of plenty, now missing. He is clothed from the waist down, and wears boots. This Italian import in a remote German village

6.2 Schwarzenacker, Genius of the Roman People, bronze

6.3 Xanten, Bonus Eventus(?), bronze

shows how early the official cult made its way to the provinces. At a way station on an important trunk highway, visitors from the metropolis on official business would be frequent, and would expect to see evidence of native piety toward official cult. This statuette was part of that evidence; other statuettes found in the same cellar, of Apollo, Neptune, Victory, and Mercury, reinforce the impression.

Another imported bronze, this time life-size, fished out of the Rhine near Xanten, may provide further evidence of Roman cult in Germany, if it represents, as has been plausibly conjectured, Bonus Eventus, the god of good result, whether in crops or any other human activity. He is represented (Fig. 6.3) as a boy in his early teens, with outstretched arms. Since his effeminate air closely resembles statues of the Emperor Hadrian's boy-love Antinous,* he has been dated about A.D. 130. Whether he came from a temple or a villa, he is evidence of close religious connection with the homeland kept up by the Roman Establishment on a far frontier.

The Jupiter-column in Mainz, described in an earlier chapter, shows, as we saw, how Roman and native deities were amalgamated. Numbers of such columns survive. One from Weissenhof is now in the Landesmuseum in Stuttgart (Fig. 6.4). It represents a bearded god (Jupiter to the Romans, the native sky-god Taranis, Donar, or Ziu to the Germans) riding roughshod over a monster or giant whose lower limbs tail away into something fishlike. These figures presumably represent the triumph of civilization over barbarism. The columns on which they stand usually rest on a two-level pedestal. The lower, four-sided, portrays in

* *The Mute Stones Speak*, p. 283ff.; paperback, pp. 279ff.

6.4 Weissenhof, Jupiter-giant statue

relief either Juno, Mercury, Hercules, or Minerva, symbolizing marriage, commerce, transport, and handicrafts, or,
according to other authorities, the four seasons. Above
these is a seven-sided plinth representing the Germanic
days of the week: Sol–Sonntag, etc. The Weissenhof sculpture is of local stone, carved by a native sculptor, probably
in the early third century A.D. By this time local bene-
ficiaries of the Roman peace were apparently willing to
express their gratitude for its blessings by symbolizing in
terms of their own religious iconography the suppression
of the more recalcitrant element among them by the
Roman ruling power.

Most of the area where what we may call the Niebelung-
Wagnerian divinities were worshiped (Wotan, Thor, Freya,
and the rest) lay north and east of the Limes, renounced
by Rome after the debacle of the Teutoburg Forest. But
sporadic evidence does turn up of the worship of these
Teutonic gods in Roman Germany. One example is a
crude native sandstone relief of a god holding a hammer
(Fig. 6.5) found in the Imperial Baths in Trier, which
were built in the late third century A.D. He could be the

**6.5 Trier, hammer-god, relief**

Teutonic Donar, Norse Thor, who made the thunder by hammering on his anvil. To the Romans, who tried to reduce their own confusion about native deities by equating them with their own, the hammer-god was either Vulcan the smith or Jupiter the wielder of the thunderbolt. The problem of identification is complicated by the fact that the Celts too had a hammer-god, whom they called Sucellus, and our relief was found in Celtic territory. The Romans equated Sucellus with Silvanus, god of uncultivated woodlands. But whether Germanic or Celtic, this relief by a native sculptor of a native god, found in a Roman context, in an area that had been Roman for 300 years, is significant evidence of the long survival of local cult in an urban and sophisticated setting.

Compared to the scanty evidence for the worship of Teutonic gods in Roman Germany, testimony for Celtic divinities is much more widespread. For example, a well in a sanctuary of Mercury (according to Tacitus the German's favorite deity: he was the god of trade and gain) excavated in 1844 at Finthen, four miles west of Mainz, yielded a gilt bronze female head (Fig. 6.6), plausibly identified as that of the Celtic goddess Rosmerta, consort of Mercury, and equated by the Romans with his mother Maia, a goddess of fertility and abundance. In style, the bust is a competent provincial imitation of Roman work of the middle third of the second century A.D. Since this bust of a Celtic goddess, presumably commissioned by a worshiper or worshipers of Celtic stock, can stand by itself as a work of art, which is more than can be said for the Jupiter-giant sculpture, or the hammer-god from Trier, the conclusion appears warranted that the Celtic population of Roman Germany was both more prosperous, and, from the Roman point of view, more civilized, than the Germanic.

6.6  Mainz, Rosmerta, bronze bust

Our next Celtic example is not a work of art but a 350-foot-square temple precinct, that of Lenus-Mars, across the Mosel from Trier (Fig. 6.7). It rose in the last half of the second century A.D. over a spring whose waters had healing properties. It was planned as a series of terraces, like the Hellenistic Greek healing sanctuary of Asclepius on the Aegean island of Cos, or the main temple at Baalbek in Syria. The approach was by a broad flight of steps, across a long portico with Corinthian columns, into a court, from which two further flights of stairs led to the temple itself, set axially symmetrical at the back of the precinct. The central part of the temple terrace projected like the apron of a stage, and its balustraded front wall was faced with reliefs, and surmounted by columns supporting statues. At the top of the central stair was, as usual, the altar, which in Roman temples was never inside. The monotony of the back courtyard wall, to the left and right of the apron, was relieved by a series of engaged Ionic pilasters. Two arched entrances on either side gave access to rooms where temple gear was stored. The temple terrace was flanked, in the native manner, by low porticoes, with statues between the columns. The temple itself had a double colonnade on each side, with statues of Victories atop pillars beyond the outside corners of each. The temple architrave bore a dedicatory inscription to Lenus-Mars and Ancamna (the Celtic goddess of Victory). The ridgepole and corners of the pediment (*acroteria*) bore animal figures. The columns of the temple, on their sculptured plinths, were, like most of the columns in the precinct, Corinthian, the most ornate of the three orders of Graeco-Roman architecture, and the one preferred by the Romans. The whole effect, executed in white marble, is a tribute to a Celtic god in Graeco-Roman architectural language of the last half of the second century A.D. And the reconstruction, from rather unlikely fragments, is a tribute to the ingenuity of the excavators.

The Celtic protectress of horses, Epona—whose name is

6.7 Trier, Lenus-Mars temple, reconstruction drawing

related to Latin *equus;* "horse"—was worshiped all over the horse-rearing provinces of Belgica and Germania Superior: over fifty representations of her are known. One from Köngen (Fig. 6.8), near Stuttgart, is now in the Stuttgart museum. The goddess is dressed like a countrywoman, with an apron. She is seated with a basket of feed in her lap, and is flanked, heraldically, by a pair of horses. Another Stuttgart relief shows her with as many as eight horses, and she is often shown sitting sidesaddle. It is reasonable to suppose that her worship was spread by Celtic cavalry-men serving as auxiliaries in the Roman army. Köngen was a *castellum* on the Odenwald-Neckar Limes, before Antoninus Pius moved the frontier eastward. The experts date the relief to the end of the second or the beginning of the third century A.D. It was therefore dedicated not by soldiers but by the civilian population of Köngen.

6.8 Köngen, Epona, relief

Another set of Celtic goddesses whose worship was wide-spread in Roman Germany were the *Matronae*. Over 700 monuments dedicated to them are known. They are usually represented as a trinity, seated under a canopy, holding baskets of fruit in their laps, which suggests that their worship had something to do with the fertility and prosperity of the family. Different tribes and localities worshiped the Matronae under a tongue-twisting variety of epithets. A whole set of Matronae-inscriptions turned up in 1928-1929 in the course of excavations under the Münster in Bonn. About A.D. 400 the Christians of the Bonn community were moved to build a chapel over the site of the martyrdom of two of their number. For the building-stones of their chapel they chose pagan monuments, hacked to convenient size, and among them was one of the most impressive of the Matronae-dedications (Fig. 6.9), made

6.9 Bonn, Matronae, relief

in the late second or early third century by one Q. Vettius Severus, a Roman official in Köln, to the Matronae Aufaniae. The Matronae sit on a curved, cushioned bench, bearing in their laps the canonical baskets of fruit. The central figure is an adolescent girl; the flanking figures wear the remarkable teased coiffures characteristic of these deities. The smaller figures peering over the back of the bench are presumably humans, the family of the dedicator.

For Matronae-worship the evidence includes sanctuaries as well as individual monuments. The most elaborate was excavated in the middle twenties in the Altbach valley, in the south quarter of Trier (Fig. 6.10). It measures nearly 1,000 feet on a side, and contained some seventy shrines, priests' houses, and temples, large and small, many of the Celtic type, simple, square, and surrounded by a low portico, but some round, like the Mercury chapel (plan, 2), and some simpler still, a roof supported by four posts over a sacred spot. The Matronae had a sanctuary here (plan, 5), and there was a theater, presumably for the performance of mystery plays with a religious significance.

A large number of terracotta masks, used in these plays, was found in fragments on the site. A similar mask (Fig. 6.11) was found whole at Worms (the ancient Barbetomagus). Below the ears are holes for the strings that fastened it to the face. The wrinkled forehead, staring eyes, wart, crooked nose, grimacing smile, and jagged teeth are well calculated to amuse adults and frighten children. Similar ones from the temple of Artemis Orthia at Sparta * served similar cult purposes. Indeed, there is a further analogy with Greece, for the many-buildinged sanctuary in Trier has been aptly compared by the German excavators, for complexity, with the great Greek international shrines at Delphi and Olympia. Trier, too, was an important tribal religious center from at least the time of the Roman con-

* See *The Greek Stones Speak*, Fig. 3.16.

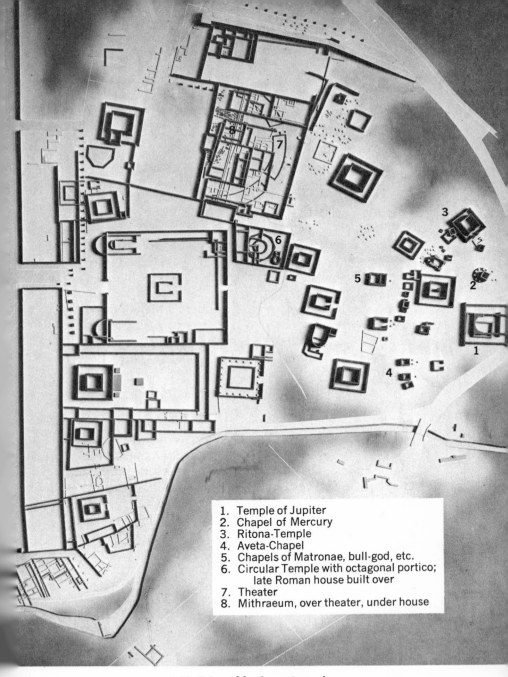

1. Temple of Jupiter
2. Chapel of Mercury
3. Ritona-Temple
4. Aveta-Chapel
5. Chapels of Matronae, bull-god, etc.
6. Circular Temple with octagonal portico;
   late Roman house built over
7. Theater
8. Mithraeum, over theater, under house

6.10 Trier, Altbach precinct, plan

quest, and its cultic importance may have influenced its choice as a Roman capital in the late Empire. The Altbach precinct was destroyed twice, once in the Batavian uprising in A.D. 70, and again by the Christians in the fourth century.

A sanctuary excavated beginning in 1912 at Pesch, in the Eifel some twenty-four miles southwest of Bonn, was identified by inscriptions as sacred to the Matronae. Excavation was complicated by the fact that the land belonged to ten different owners, and the news that archaeologists were interested caused prices to rise excessively. The excavation trenches had to be narrow, in order to spare the trees. Careful attention to stratigraphy, and to finds of coins, made it possible to identify three phases in the sanctuary, of which the first went back to Nero's reign (*ca.* A.D. 50), the second extended from A.D. 200 to 330, and the third and most flourishing (see model, Fig. 6.12) from 330 to about 400. The precinct was bounded on three sides by a fence; on the fourth (east) by a covered walkway a hundred yards long, half-timbered on the outer face, and supported by wooden columns. The half-timbering testifies to the rustic quality of the sanctuary. The building at the near end of the walkway had two rooms: one the sacristan's quarters; the other, a rest room for pilgrims, held Matronae-altars and inscriptions. The other half-timbered building was perhaps a priest's house. At the midpoint of the walkway was a well forty-three feet deep, found full of altars, sculpture, architectural members, inscriptions, and the wood of the wellhead. The building at the north end of the sanctuary (model, right) is a typical Gallo-Roman temple, square, and surrounded by a low portico, like the ones already mentioned in the Altbach sanctuary in Trier. In it was found a statue of Jupiter, with his eagle, and a laurel crown. The open-air precinct to the south of the temple held altars, statues of Matronae, inscriptions built into the walls, and a statue that has been identified as

**170**

6.11  Worms, comic mask, terra-cotta


6.12  Pesch, temple precinct, model

Cybele, the Asiatic Great Mother of the gods. The hexagonal shrine, its columns finished in a fish-scale pattern, sheltered a statue of Jupiter. The building restored in the model with a clerestory was originally thought to be a basilica, a festival hall for Matronae-worshipers, but recent excavation has shown that the footings of the columns do not go down to bedrock. They would therefore not have supported two stories, and the building should be restored with a flat roof. The columns in question are Corinthian, with cases and cupboards between, separating the nave from the side aisles. Around the red-painted walls were statue-bases and benches.

It is noteworthy how in this sanctuary the gods of three cultures lived comfortably and tolerantly together: the Celtic Matronae, the Roman Jupiter, the Asiatic Greek Cybele. By the fourth century, when the sanctuary was in its prime, the three cultures were so blended in the province, having lived together for so long, that a worshiper, whatever his background, would feel nothing strange about paying homage to any one of the three. This non-segregation was for Germans a major blessing of the Roman peace.

The Celts worshiped totem animals. Charming evidence for such a cult is provided by a small bronze discovered in the eighteenth century at Muri, just southeast of Bern, and

**6.13 Muri, goddess Artio, with bear, bronze statuette**

now in the Historical Museum there (Fig. 6.13). Its inscription identifies the female figure as Artio. She was the bear-goddess, as the sculptor has indicated rather forcibly in the huge lumbering animal who faces her on the pedestal. It is appropriate that the piece should be housed in Bern, for this is the bear-city in the bear-canton, with a bear on its flag and pet bears kept in a pit for the delectation of visitors.

Ideas and men traveled easily and quickly across the Roman Empire. Greek-speaking soldiers were assigned to the German provinces; Greek-speaking traders came there to capitalize on provincial prosperity. They brought their cults with them. One of the weirdest was the cult of Jupiter Sabazius (the Sabaoth of the Jews). Sabazius was a divinity at home in two of the most barbarous areas of the Greek East: Thrace (nowadays Bulgaria) and Phrygia in northwest Asia Minor. Evidence for his worship comes from a series of votive hands. The one illustrated (Fig. 6.14) was found in Avenches, and is dated in the second century A.D. It is in bronze, and represents the hand of the god himself, raised in benediction. The hand is encrusted with an unappetizing collection of objects: busts of gods, cult paraphernalia, and good-luck charms. Balanced on the point of the thumb is a pine cone, a fertility symbol. At the back of the thumb, seen in profile in the illustration, is a bust of Cybele, the Asiatic Mother Goddess, wearing a mural crown. Between the raised first two fingers is the bust of Sabazius himself, wearing the pointed Phrygian cap. Below him is a round loaf of bread scored for breaking into quarters. On the back of the fingers, invisible in the photograph, is a figure of Bacchus dancing. Perched on the knuckles of the third and fourth fingers is a bust of Mercury, identified by his winged hat. Behind it a ram's head,

6.14 Avenches, votive hand of Sabazius, bronze

facing a frog, behind the frog a lizard, beside the lizard a branch of oak. On the wrist is a bell; below the bell, twined about the wrist, is a snake. A subjective judgment, that this is a repulsive and tasteless object, is obviously culture-bound. It amounts to a recognition that the Roman Empire was a melting pot, in which a significant number of human beings held beliefs far removed indeed from the orthodox Graeco-Roman ones we read about in Greek and Latin literature, and which we accept as part of the foundation of our culture. And, if we strip away the accretions, the Sabazius-cult has affinities familiar to us: the gesture of benediction by the votive hand is exactly the same as that made by the Pope when he blesses the faithful assembled in their thousands in St. Peter's Square.

Cybele is figured on the votive hand, and her name has come up frequently in our discussion. Cybele in mythology has a lover, the young Attis, whom she forced to castrate himself to prevent his marriage to another. In honor of Attis, the priests of Cybele castrated themselves and served her as eunuchs. A typical statuette of Attis, fished out of the Mosel by the Roman bridge at Trier, was published in

1964 (Fig. 6.15). He is figured as a chubby, effeminate child (as yet uncastrated) wearing the pointed Phrygian cap on his curly head, and a one-piece trousered costume buttoned down the front of the legs with inlaid buttons, and open to reveal the private parts and stomach. Again, hardly to the Queen's taste, but obviously very much to the taste of hundreds of votaries who no doubt saw in Attis an impulse to chastity different only in degree, not in kind, from the vows taken by Christian priests and nuns.

The patron saint of Syrians serving in the Roman army was Jupiter Dolichenus, the Semitic god Baal as worshiped in Doliche, in the hinterland of Syria. A late-second-century

**6.15 Trier, Attis, bronze**

6.16 Heddernheim, Jupiter Dolichenus, bronze plaque

bronze plaque found in the Roman *castellum* at Heddernheim, a suburb of Frankfurt, is to be seen in the Wiesbaden
museum (Fig. 6.16). Its details exemplify the intermingling
of Near Eastern religions with one another and with
Roman. It is shaped like a spear point. At the top is the
sun, with a headdress of his own rays. Next below flies
Victory, carrying palm branch and leafy crown. The central
figure is the bearded Dolichenus himself, schizophrenically
dressed in Roman uniform, but with Phrygian trousers. His
right hand brandishes a double-ax, his left a six-pronged
thunderbolt. He is standing on a bull. In the lower register
the central figure is the Egyptian goddess Isis, in typical
headdress. She stands upon a doe, and holds in her right

**176**

hand her rattle (*sistrum*), in her left a scepter.* Flanking
her are a pair of giants, also in Roman uniform, but their
legs tailing away into spirals. They hold aloft three-pronged
plants, perhaps lilies. On their heads are busts of the moon,
in crescent headdress, and the sun, radiate, as at the top of
the plaque. The gods of Syria, Egypt, and Rome are
blended here, and the double representation of the radiate
sun is an allusion to the divinity most popular of all among
the soldiers: Mithras, the Persian god of light.

Mithras was the object of the most widespread Oriental
cult in Roman Germany: a recent collection of Mithraic
monuments there runs to nearly 400 items. Mithras was
especially popular with Greek soldiers in the Roman army,
and with Asiatic traders. His worship was secret, carried on
in underground rooms simulating caves. These had benches
along the walls, and at the end an altar (we have seen how
un-Roman it is to have an altar *inside* a place of worship),
with sculpture and/or reliefs of scenes from Mithras' life.
The initiates went through seven stages of initiation, like
the degrees in Freemasonry, each with its appropriate symbol: Crow, Bridegroom, Soldier, Lion, Persian, Sun-runner,
and Father, or Worshipful Master.† Votaries of Mithras
believed that being washed in the blood of a freshly slaughtered bull brought redemption and immortality.

The details of Mithras' life and legend are revealed in
reliefs found in various Mithraea. One of the best examples
was found in 1926 by workmen digging a cellar in Dieburg,

* There is a good deal of evidence for the worship of Egyptian deities
in Roman Germany. For example, there was found at Obertraubling, just
southeast of Regensburg, a bronze Apis (Fig. 6.17), now in the Regensburg museum. Apis was the sacred bull, incarnation of the god Ptah at
Egyptian Memphis, and patron of smiths and sculptors. When a sacred
bull died, he was mummified, and mourned for seventy days. Archaeologists
have found a whole cemetery of sacred bulls at Memphis. The Roman
authorities officially recognized the cult, and it will have been brought to
the Danube by Egyptian auxiliaries in the Roman army.

† See *The Mute Stones Speak*, pp. 263-4; paperback, pp. 259-260, 262
(Ostia).

6.17 Regensburg, Apis, bronze

twenty miles south of Frankfurt. It was excavated, with
commendable *esprit de corps*, by the alumni of the local
classical high school or *Gymnasium*. It is a relief in red
sandstone, carved on both sides, and arranged to revolve
on a pivot. It is now in the local museum in Dieburg. It is
dated on stylistic grounds in the last third of the second
century A.D. The Mithraeum from which it came was apparently destroyed in the Alemannic invasion of A.D. 260.
Dieburg lies well behind the line of the Limes, which runs
fifteen miles to the east: the Mithraic congregation there
was therefore civilian, not military. The dedicators of the
relief have inscribed their occupations: one was the sculptor
himself, the other a cobbler. Their fellow worshipers may
have included well-to-do Romans like the proprietor of a
villa of the second or third century, discovered in 1968 at
Gross-Umstadt nearby.

The front of the relief (Fig. 6.18) is divided into eleven

178

panels. The details of the interpretation are controversial, but the cult story emerges quite clearly. We begin at the bottom, to the left of the inscription, where we have two animals, horses or goats, facing in opposite directions. Proceeding clockwise, we see a naked bearded figure seated on a rock, holding a dagger. He might be Saturn or Hercules, but the most attractive interpretation is that he is Ahriman, lord of darkness, Mithras' inveterate enemy, with whom he struggles for the possession of men's souls. Next above is Mithras being born from a cliff; he holds a torch in one hand and a dagger in the other. In the fourth panel Mithras in a Phrygian cap is reaping grain, which worshipers believed sprang from the blood of the slaughtered bull. In the broken upper left corner Mithras is climbing a tree. In the double panel at the top, Mithras, with a stone in his hand, frees the sacrificial bull, whose tail ends in a wheatear. The bull is imprisoned in a temple-like building in whose pediment the Raven (one of the degrees of initia-

**6.18 Dieburg, Mithras relief, obverse**

tion) is flanked by the heads of the moon and the sun. (The Raven bore from the Sun-god to Mithras the order to kill the bull.) At the right of this triptych-panel Mithras trudges off with the bull over his shoulder. In the upper right corner the bull is putting up a fight, trying to drag Mithras away, but in the next panel Mithras has overcome, and has again slung the bull over his shoulder. Below is a tree with three branches, each adorned with a head in a Phrygian cap. The heads probably represent Mithras flanked by Cautes and Cautopates, the rising and the setting sun. In the lower right corner Mithras and the Sun, drinking-horns in hand, toast each other, using the slaughtered bull's hide as their banquet tablecloth. The eleventh small panel shows Mithras being carried up into heaven in the four-horse chariot of the Sun. The large central panel is a hunting scene. Mithras, on horseback, with flying cloak, Phrygian cap, and bow and arrow, pursues a hare, with the enthusiastic assistance of a trio of large hunting dogs. In the corners are Cautes and Cautopates, perched upon wine-bowls.

The back of the relief represents, uniquely among Mithraic monuments, the myth of the fiery end of the world through the agency of Phaethon-Mithras (Fig. 6.19). In the center is the Sun-god enthroned; to the left his son Phaethon asking his father for the fatal loan of his chariot. Four young squires lead the horses for harnessing; the four female figures are the four seasons. In the background is the temple of the Sun, with Corinthian columns, and a medallion of the sun in the middle of the pediment. Below the steps of the throne are three of the four elements. The central bearded figure with the vault of heaven over his head is Air. The right-hand figure, with the horn of plenty, is Earth; on the left, with a jug, is Water. The Sun himself, of course, is the fourth element, Fire.

6.19 Dieburg, Mithras relief, reverse

To the Romans, Christianity was just another Near Eastern religion. In Germany, Christian worship centered in the Rhine and Mosel valleys, and was already strong in the fourth century A.D. Part of the Christian symbolism was the dove of peace, as represented in a fourth-century bronze lamp found at Altrip on the Rhine below Ludwigshafen, and now in the Speyer museum (Fig. 6.20).

There is archaeological evidence for Christianity at all the major sites we have discussed so far: along the Rhine from Xanten to Augst; also at Windisch and Avenches, and at Trier. One of the earliest monuments is the oratory and cemetery under the present Gothic church of St. Severin in Köln, on the Roman military road to Bonn. Excavation there before and after World War II established that, between A.D. 160 and 180, Christian burials began to appear in the pagan cemetery, which had been in

**6.20 Altrip, dove-lamp, bronze**

use since the third quarter of the first century A.D. Christian graves can be identified by the method of burial (Christians avoided cremation), by the Chi-Rho monogram (the first two letters of the name of Christ in Greek), by the appearance of symbolic figures like the Good Shepherd, and by the occurrence on gravestones of characteristic Christian names like Concordia. About A.D. 320 an altar, enclosed in a modest oratory, rose over two particular graves. These will have been of martyrs. The most famous example of a cemetery, originally pagan, then Christian, with a church on the site of the martyrdom is to be found in the excavations under St. Peter's in Rome,* where Constantine's church is of the same date as the more modest building in Köln. About A.D. 400 the Köln oratory was enlarged by the addition of a room on each side and a

---

* See *The Mute Stones Speak*, pp. 340-350; paperback, pp. 335-344.

Other Gods Than Ours

vestibule or narthex. A grave chamber in the narthex is believed by some to have been the last resting place of one of Köln's early bishops, St. Severinus, after whom the present church is named. At the end of the fifth century the church was enlarged again, with additions front and back. This is the phase shown in the model (Fig. 6.21). It is in the characteristic construction style of the period, with a course of brick laid between every three courses of stone. Its clerestory is borrowed from the pagan Roman basilica; its low side rooms are borrowed from the typical Gallo-Roman temple, so that this Christian monument gives evidence for the mingling of cultures, for the syncretism, which we have found to be typical of other Near Eastern religions in Roman Germany. In the sixth or seventh century a cloister was added to the west. The foundations of the present church go back to Charlemagne, with remodelings in 948 and later, so that St. Severin may be taken as yet another example of unbroken continuity in Roman Germany from the early Empire to the Middle Ages.

**6.21 Köln, St. Severin, model**

# 7 : Arts and Crafts
# Beyond the Alps

So far we have been discussing the archaeological evidence of Roman artifacts and buildings for the light they throw on history (Chapters 1 through 4), economic life (Chapter 5), and religion (Chapter 6). In this chapter we shall concentrate largely on selected archaeological evidence for the Romans in Germany as technicians, and as teachers of their techniques to Germans. The evidence comes from a variety of fields: architecture, sculpture in stone and bronze, work in clay, hydraulics, surgery, wine-making, and work in mosaic. Since every good craftsman is in a sense an artist, we shall find that some of the products of Greek, Roman, or native techniques in Germany can stand in their own right as works of art, and we shall therefore illustrate some objects of intrinsic aesthetic value above and beyond what they contribute to the history of technology and to other fields.

We begin with architecture. Many of the buildings in Roman Germany were planned to use blocks of stone too large to raise by hand. To meet the difficulty, the Romans made use of the block and tackle, the principle of which they had learned from the Greeks, who in turn learned it from the Egyptians. Egyptian priests told the Greek historian Herodotus that block and tackle were used in the construction of the Great Pyramid at Gizeh, which dates from near the beginning of the Fourth Dynasty, about 2,600 B.C. No examples of Roman block-and-tackle cranes have actually been found in Germany, but the existence of buildings and walls made of large blocks shows that they must have been used, and the DEMAG firm in Duisburg built a model that was displayed in 1967 in the Köln exposition, "Römer am Rhein" (Fig. 7.1). The model is based on a Flavian relief of about A.D. 75 from the tomb of the Haterii, now in the Lateran collection in Rome, and on the description in Vitruvius, who wrote, as we saw, in the time of Augustus. So we may imagine that such cranes were used, for example, in erecting the walls and public buildings of the Colonia Agrippinensium, modern Köln.

Vitruvius describes a crane for which two long pieces of timber are set up, connected at the top with a brace, spreading at the bottom, and supported by ropes. At the top is a block containing two pulleys (in the model, three) revolving on axles. The leading rope is passed over the top pulley, then let down and drawn round a pulley of the lower block. It is returned to the middle pulley of the top block, then passed to the middle pulley of the lower block, and so on, alternating, until it is fastened to an eye in the lower block. On the back face of the upright timbers, near the bottom, axle-sockets are fixed. The ropes from the pulleys are wound round the axle, and it is revolved by men working a treadmill. Iron pincers suspended from the lower pulley-block fit into holes previously drilled in the stone to be raised. The use of six pulleys means that a load can be lifted by the application of a force only one-sixth as large. The model illustrates, at a scale of 1:20, a crane that could lift loads of six tons.

7.1  Roman block and tackle, model

Sculpture in stone was a technique the finer points of which the Germans learned from the Romans, as the Romans had learned it from the Greeks. Since marble is not native to Germany, and is too heavy to transport easily by land in the block, the assumption is that any marble statues in Germany were imported from Italy. The sculptor's tools, as today, were chisels—straight-edged, rounded, pointed, or toothed—drill, rasp, file, and mallet. Marble was given a gloss finish by rubbing it with pumice, sand, or emery, or even by coating it with wax, though purists frowned on the latter procedure, since it might be used to cover imperfections in a flawed stone. (The English word "sincere" is said by some to be derived from the Latin *sine cera*, "without wax.") Statues were not dead-white, but colored, with inlaid or painted eyes.

The head in Figure 7.2, found in Mainz in 1961 and now in the Mittelrheinisches Landesmuseum there, is of white marble, carefully finished and polished; it originally had painted eyes. It was published as the likeness of Augustus' grandson Gaius, but the treatment of the hair is so like that in the most famous statue of Augustus—he affected a hair style like that of Alexander the Great—that scholarly opinion now inclines to see here the young Augustus, dedicated after his death by loyal citizens of one of Germany's chief centers.

Our next example (Fig. 7.3) of sculpture in stone was found in Köln in the eighteenth century. It is of white, fine-grained marble, and has suffered badly from miscon-

**7.2 Mainz, head of Augustus, marble**

7.3 Köln, Agrippina the Younger, marble

ceived restoration for display purposes. The nose, for example, has been restored, and the surface has been merci-
lessly cleaned. Traces of the painted eyes, however, are
still visible, and we can see the way the ringlets have been
rendered with the drill. This technique was in vogue in
Rome about A.D. 140, though the subject—identified from
the likeness to coin-portraits—is Agrippina the Younger,
the foundress of Köln, who died eighty years before this
statue was carved.

Our third marble head (Fig. 7.4) was found in 1908 in
Schwarzrheindorf, on the Rhine opposite the Roman camp
at Bonn. The coiffure is identical with that affected by
Faustina the Elder, wife of Antoninus Pius (reigned A.D.
138-161), and aunt of Marcus Aurelius. It was intended for

**7.4 Bonn, Faustina the Elder, marble**

insertion into a marble body. We have already mentioned the use of detachable heads as an economy measure. The head is highly polished, and the sculptor used the drill for the pupils of the eyes. Ancient critics questioned Faustina's character, and modern ones have not failed to see that character reflected in this portrait: dull eyes, fleshy nose, mean mouth, weak chin. But this is a highly subjective judgment. It is equally possible to see in this portrait the sensitive woman whose marriage was harmonious, and whose husband endowed a charitable foundation in her name.

The three examples of stone sculpture discussed so far have been in marble, and Italian in influence if not in origin. The next is provincial. It is a sandstone sarcophagus (Fig. 7.5) of about A.D. 150, found in 1930 in Simpelveld in the extreme south of the Netherlands, just northwest of Aachen, and now in the Leyden museum. It belongs to the realm where the stone cutter and the sculptor meet, and is more interesting as a unique document than as a work of art. It is, as Lady Brogan well says in her book on Roman Gaul, "designed not to be a monument for the passer-by to admire, but to be company for the deceased," for the sculpture is all on the inside of the sarcophagus. It portrays the departed, a lady, lying on a handsome cushioned and paneled couch with lathe-turned legs. From her corner, she has a view of her whole comfortable domain: basket-chair, wardrobe, a chest with demijohns of wine on top, a console table with lion's-foot legs, shelves of wine pitchers and other containers, a commode with paneled doors, a niche for cult-statue (perhaps of Mithras), and, in the far corner, a shrine with five niches: perhaps her household gods, the Lares and Penates, reposed below, and the Capitoline triad, Jupiter, Juno, and Minerva, above. Other niches for her gods are carved at the foot of the sarcophagus, and at the foot of her couch the stonecutter has rendered two of the buildings of her estate. There is no more vivid

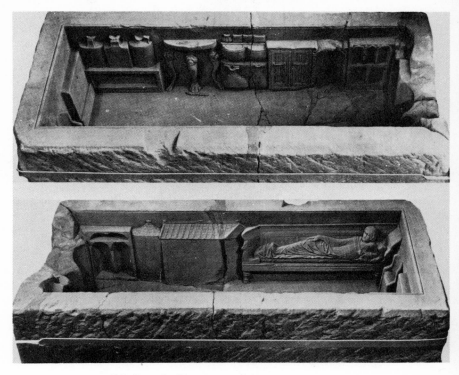

7.5 Simpelveld, stone sarcophagus

picture in existence of comfortable bourgeois life in Lower Germany in the palmiest days of Roman Imperial prosperity.

Our final example of provincial sculpture in stone comes from the vast graveyard in Regensburg, and dates from the late second or early third century A.D. It is a lion (Fig. 7.6), crudely carved in local stone. Lions are not indigenous to Raetia, so the inspiration is foreign (a symbol of the triumph of death), though the workmanship is provincial. The beast amuses visitors to the Regensburg museum because of its uncanny likeness to a prominent post-World War II East German politician.

7.6 Regensburg, stone lion

Sculpture in bronze is another Graeco-Roman technique not native to Germany, and most German examples are imports: bronze, being hollow, is much more portable than marble. The commonest technique is the so-called "lost wax" process. The sculpture is done first in clay, then thinly coated with wax. Over the wax the sculptor daubs an outer coat of clay. The photograph (Fig. 7.7), taken in a bronze-caster's workshop in Rome, illustrates this stage of the process. He then through a tube pours in molten bronze, which replaces the wax. Other tubes allow for the wax and exhaust vapors to flow out, and for the metal to be poured in at various points to allow for uniform cooling. The outer coat of clay is then broken off, the clay core removed and what is left is a thin bronze shell that the sculptor then retouches, using an engraving tool called a

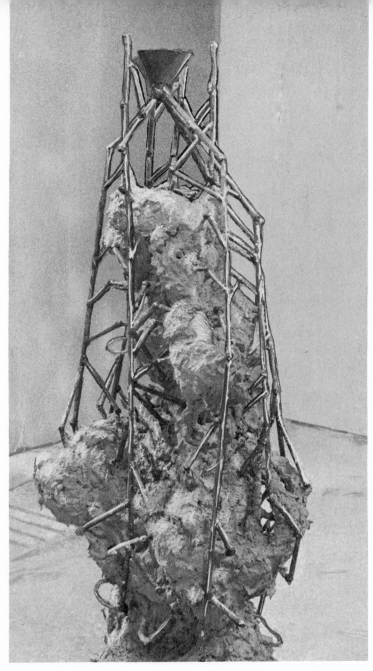

7.7 Bronze-casting by lost-wax process

burin Sometimes he adds gilding, and insets the eyes in glass paste.

One of the finest examples of Roman bronze sculpture in Germany is a bust (Fig. 7.8) from the *castellum* at Rheingönheim, opposite the mouth of the Neckar, now in the museum at Speyer. Its date can be narrowed down by historical and artistic data. The fort from which it came was manned from Claudius to Vespasian (A.D. 41-79), and a bust very much like it was found in a house in Pompeii, which was destroyed by Vesuvius in A.D. 79. Since the bust came from a Roman fort, it must represent a prominent member of the Roman Establishment, but exact identification has become a scholarly game with no outcome; one can only name the candidates: Tiberius' prefect Sejanus, Mark Antony, Augustus' lieutenant Agrippa, Augustus' grandson Gaius, and Domitius Ahenobarbus, Antony's son-in-law and Augustus' grandnephew, who at least had connections with Germany: he marched from the Danube to the Elbe, and built a causeway across the marshes between the Rhine and the Ems.

Our next example (Fig. 7.9) is a gilt bronze head of a barbarian, from Avenches, dated on grounds of style in the mid-second century A.D. The impression it gives is "strong," a term used by modern sculptors of pieces they are not sure they like. The stringy hair, half-closed eyes, slack, sad, downturned lips, and heavy chin produce a Caliban-like effect unique in ancient sculpture. Whether the artist was sympathetic with his subject or not, he has made a statement about the lot of the downtrodden in the Roman Empire that is much at variance with the rosy view of prosperity and widespread happiness derived from over-concentration on spas, luxury villas, and the grave-furniture of the rich

Another bronze from Avenches is the statuette of a

7.8 Rheingönheim, bust of Roman dignitary, bronze

195

7.9 Avenches, head of barbarian, gilt bronze

squatting, potbellied Silenus (Fig. 7.10): in mythology, the companion on his revels of the wine-god Bacchus. The sculptor has made the little god deliberately grotesque, taking great pains with the hair on his private parts, around his nipples, and in his armpit. The finger-like appendage in his back is to hang him up by. Such bibelots were fashionable under the Severan dynasty, and this piece is therefore dated on stylistic grounds between A.D. 200 and 225.

Perhaps the most charming bronze in all Germany is the delightful head of a small boy found in Speyer and now in the Hessisches Landesmuseum in Darmstadt. The illustration (Fig. 7.11) shows how the top of the skull has been restored. The sculptor, a genius, has caught the touching immaturity of young boyhood perfectly, by a realistic rendition of the big head and ears, the undeveloped features, and the thin neck. We do not normally associate a love for small children with the Romans, but we should, for there is much evidence for it in Roman art and literature. Modern Italians inherit their affection for the young from the Romans, wrongly stereotyped as dour and unfeeling.

Germans under Roman tutelage became quite adept at the potter's craft. Figure 7.12 shows a potter's kiln at Kobern on the north bank of the Mosel near Koblenz. It must be mentally reconstructed with a fire-room below and a beehive vault above. In the fire room, clay flues led from the fire to each of the holes visible in the photograph.

**7.10 Avenches, Silenus, bronze statuette**

The pots, after being decorated and turned ("thrown") on the wheel, were placed in the kiln for firing, on an iron grid just above the holes.

Germans made passable imitations of the fine Roman red-glazed and embossed ware (imitating originals in silver) called Arretine, from Arezzo in Tuscany, where it was first made. One of the major German pottery centers was Rhein-zabern (Tabernae), ten miles south of Speyer (Novio-magus). Most of what we know about German pottery results from the tireless labors of a devoted amateur, him-self a pottery manufacturer, Wilhelm Ludovici, who gathered over a span of forty-five years (1884-1929) and published in five volumes at his own expense the most complete collection in existence of Rheinzabern pottery stamps—nearly 13,000 items. These stamps, bearing the Latinized names of German potters, make it possible to date and to trace the distribution of Rheinzabern pottery, and thus to write an important chapter in the economic history of Roman Germany from A.D. 130, when the kilns were at their peak of production, to 260, when the Aleman-nic invaders destroyed them.

The Germanic imitations, like the Italian originals, were

7.11  Speyer, head of boy, bronze

199

made from clay molds, in which concave hand stamps made negative impressions that emerged convex in the final vase. Besides the potter's name, the patterns on the stamps included rosettes, bead and reel, egg and dart, gods, gladiators, charioteers, masks, animals, birds, fish, monsters, palmettes, and many others. The German potters never quite succeeded in reproducing the handsome metallic red glaze of the Italian originals, which was produced by dipping the pots in a special thin slip of sodium carbonate or silicate. The German ceramic expert Theodor Schumann rediscovered the secret in 1942.

One of the handsomest and earliest examples of imported Italian ware in Germany comes from the Augustan camp at Haltern, which, as we saw, must be dated very early in the first century A.D. It is the so-called "Aco-beaker" (Fig. 7.13) named from the potter's stamp, Acastus in Latin. It is exquisitely thin-walled, and its stamped decoration includes beading, spirals, an inscription, a band of oak-leaves and acorns, and a row of arches on Corinthian columns, with palmettes between.

Potters also made figurines from molds. One of the most amusing is the caricature of a professor (Fig. 7.14), only six inches high, from Vechten in the Netherlands, near the last German Emperor's place of exile in Doorn; it is now in the provincial archaeological museum in Utrecht. The figure is dwarfish, egg-headed, and short-legged; he wears a hooded gown and holds before him his lecture notes in a scroll.

If civilization is plumbing, the Romans vie with Americans as among the most civilized people in the world. We have seen, in the aqueduct serving Köln, and in the baths, how skillful the Romans in Germany were in hydraulic engineering. A further example is a bronze water faucet

**7.13 Haltern, Aco-beaker**

**7.14 Vechten, caricature of professor, terra-cotta statuette**

(Fig. 7.15) from Petinesca, southeast of Biel in Switzerland. The faucet is noteworthy because hot and cold water flow into the same tap, to be controlled in just the right proportions, as in the most modern plumbing installations. Petinesca was a walled way-station on an important Roman road, and also a cult center, with a precinct containing seven Gallo-Roman temples and two chapels. The pilgrims were provided with all modern conveniences, including hot and cold running water.

The Romans also taught the Germans to apply the principles of hydraulics to producing music. In Budapest, ancient Aquincum, there was found in the ancient firemen's guildhall (*schola*), just outside the south gate of the Roman camp, a water-organ made of oak, elm, and figwood, a reconstruction of which is shown in Figure 7.16. An inscription on the back stated that it was a gift to the firemen by a town councilor who was also the prefect of the guild. The water-organ operates in fact by compressed air. Two pumps (visible in Figure 7.17, from the gladiator-mosaic in the villa at Nennig; the organist is playing incidental music in the arena), one on either side of the box on which the pipes rest, are operated by levers activating pistons that send a jet of air into the box. The box contains water, and an inverted funnel into which the compressed air is pumped. The water retreats before the compressed air, rises in the box, and by its weight keeps the air compressed and forces it through a pipe upwards into the wind chest, constructed between the water box and the pipes. Striking the keys activates a spring that opens or closes a slide at the bottom of each pipe, thus controlling the admission of air into it. The Budapest organ has fifty-two pipes arranged in four rows (octaves) of thirteen each, any single row of which could be played at one time, but not two rows at once. The keys representing the interval of the third are too far apart for this chord to be played: presumably Roman musical taste did not need or admire such tones.

7.15  Petinesca, bronze faucet

7.16  Budapest, water-organ, model

7.17 Nennig, water-organ, mosaic

It is pleasant to think of the Budapest firemen beguiling
their leisure by listening to this instrument.

In Roman Germany, as in Rome itself, and everywhere
else in the Empire, surgery was regarded as a craft rather
than as a profession. Doctors were usually Greek slaves,
and did not begin to have the status they enjoy in America
today. Ancient surgical instruments have turned up in the
sick bays of Roman camps in Germany, but the most complete set found to date comes from the grave of a Roman
doctor at "sweet Bingen on the Rhine" (Bingium, one of
Drusus' camps), a town seventeen miles west of Mainz,
with romantic associations: the Niebelung treasure is said
to have been buried in the Rhine near here. Our surgeon
may have been Egyptian: a bronze statuette of a hippo-

potamus with the Egyptian sacred snake on its back was found in his grave.

The instruments, now on display in the local museum, were found lying in a bronze basin used for bleeding patients. The surgeon extracted blood by creating a vacuum with cupping glasses, three of which, in bronze, were part of our surgeon's kit. They look like bells or acorns; he hung them on a bronze stand with uprights tastefully representing twining grapevines. There are scalpels with interchangeable blades, small bone spoons with a toothed edge (for cleaning the patient's ears), needle holders with socketed ends, two trephining-saws (hollow cylinders with toothed edges, for making incisions in the skull), and chisels. The photograph (Fig. 7.18) shows a retractor (for holding open the edge of a wound), an ear-spoon, a spatula, two scalpels with spatulas at the handle end, a double-ended spatula, a probe with a curved end, a pair of pincers with a toothed grip, a curved pointed instrument perhaps for inserting in the nose to perforate and drain the

**7.18 Bingen, surgical instruments**

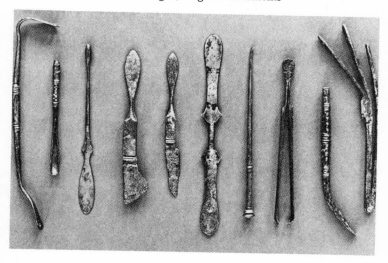

sinus, and a double-hinged instrument, described as a "trephining-bow," but possibly used to clamp off sections of the bowel. The implications of this set of instruments are forbidding, when we consider that Roman surgeons operated without the aid of anaesthetics: the Roman medical writer Celsus, in the reign of Tiberius (A.D. 14-37) advises the surgeon not to let the screams of the patient on the operating-table unsteady his hand.

Next, in this chapter of technological miscellany, we take up the archaeological evidence for wine-making, in this oinophile's paradise of Rhine and Mosel. One is glad to report that a fine pamphlet on this subject, printed in 1947 at Speyer, appeared with the enthusiastic approval of the French occupying forces, winebibbers to a man. Speyer has a fascinating wine museum, the prize exhibit of which is the world's most vintage sample of wine in a liquid state: it is 1,650 years old. Regrettably, it must be reported that the wine was proved to have been mixed with honey, and that its liquid state is due to its having been sealed with olive oil.

It is commonly reported that the Italians, wishing to monopolize the wine trade, forbade wine-making in Germany until the reign of Probus (A.D. 276-282), but pruning hooks in the Speyer museum are older than Probus. Fossils show that the vine grew wild in Germany in the Tertiary period, at least 600,000 years ago. The museum exhibits a wine-strainer from Rheinzabern, coins of Probus (a wine-lover who was murdered while laying out a vineyard), glass bottles (including one in the shape of a barrel), a wooden cask with a bung, and the cooper's good German name, Cobnertus, burned in. The German word for barrel (Fass) is a mispronunciation of Latin vas, "wine bottle." The swagger-stick carried by Roman centurions like Caelius, who died in the Teutoburg Forest (Fig. 3.14) was a vine shoot. And the Emperor Julian the Apostate (reigned A.D. 361-363), who spent long enough in Trier to become a connoisseur of Mosel wines, was moved to write in Greek an epigram against beer, in which he says that the beer-god smells of goat.

The transition from wine bottles to glassmaking is an easy one. As workers in glass, the Germans yielded to no artisans in the Empire. Köln was the center, and the museum there has a dazzling collection. The German craftsmen knew that adding various minerals to the basic mixture of sand, soda, and limestone or chalk would produce colored glass; iron oxide, at various degrees of oxidation, produced red, violet, or yellow glass; cobalt produced blue; copper oxide turned the glass red, blue, or green; zinc oxide made it milky white; manganese oxide, violet; silver chloride, a matte yellow; an admixture of gold, red. They also developed a technique for making colorless glass. The multicolored *millefiori* effect, where the various colors appear in waves or ripples, was produced by melting rods of colored glass together in patterns on a plain ground, and stretching it before blowing. Window glass was made by pouring onto a rimmed tray. Gold-ground glass resulted from laying on gold leaf, and then cutting it away to make the desired pattern. Glass was either blown or molded. Molding produced ribbed glass, glass in the shape and color of a bunch of grapes, and four-sided bottles. There are glass drinking-horns, glass vessels with colored nubs attached, and—a curiosity—a narrow-necked glass pitcher with a miniature of itself inside.

An exquisite example of the Köln glass makers' art is the tiny molded glass head (Fig. 7.19: early first century A.D.) of Augustus, just over two inches high, in the Römisch-Germanisches Museum there. Its core is blackish, with a turquoise overlay. The workmanship is as fine as a gem cutter's. The head may well have been made for insertion in a gold statuette.

7.19 Köln, miniature head of Augustus, glass

The masterpiece of the Köln collection is the cut-glass beaker illustrated in Figure 7.20. It is bell-shaped, covered with a fine network, emerald green below, yellow at the neck, with a Greek inscription, "Drink! Live well forever!" in raised ruby-red letters around the rim. The fineness of the technique that produced this masterpiece is almost incredible. The craftsman began with an ordinary molded thick-walled beaker (Fig. 7.21, 1), which he then turned

**208**

7.20 Köln, diatreta-glass beaker
7.21 Stages in cutting diatreta-glass

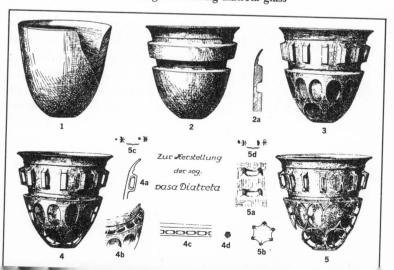

on a lathe to produce the preliminary grooves (2). He then cut the glass away, leaving rectangular projections for the letters of the inscription, and egg-shaped depressions for the network of green (3). Next, he undercut the projections, and cut away the sides of the egg-shaped depressions, leaving struts connecting the outer shell with the original core (4). Finally, he cut the edges of his network very fine, leaving x-shaped ornaments to mark his struts, and affixed the letters of the inscription (5). The delicacy of the final product is breathtaking; it is especially remarkable because it was made in a period of full decline, between A.D. 350 and 400.

Finally, we come to mosaic-making, where artist and craftsman are most nearly one. Excavation in 1874 under the north aisle of the cathedral in Trier revealed a mosaic-workshop, with a furnace for making glass cubes (*tesserae*). The glass was molded in trays, then sawed into strips, and the individual cubes knocked out of the strips with chisel and mallet. A stone block hollowed out on top served for mixing mortar. Besides glass, tesserae were made of baked clay (from broken vases), or white or colored marble. The tesserae were set in special cement, made tenacious and slow drying by mixing it with oil. For comparatively simple geometric designs, a papyrus pattern was laid directly on the floor, the pattern pricked through the paper, the paper lifted, and the tesserae laid. Lead dividers separated the panels. For more complicated figure designs, the mosaicist drew his paper pattern in reverse, covered it thinly with glue, laid his tesserae, then flipped the pattern over and applied the finished section of tesserae to the damp cement. When the tesserae had set firmly in the cement, the paper pattern could be soaked off with water. The joins between sections were filled with tesserae set directly in the cement.

An interesting combination of geometric and figured patterns was found in 1895 in the ruins of a villa of about A.D. 250 in Münster-Sarmsheim, near Bingen. It is now on display in the Rheinisches Landesmuseum in Bonn. For a room measuring sixty-two by forty-five feet, the mosaicist laid out 278 black and white geometric squares, using twelve different patterns, of which seven are shown (Fig. 7.22). Sometimes he used the same pattern with the colors reversed; for example, white triangles on a black ground instead of vice versa. The central panel, nine feet square, had its corners filled with ornate vases of different shapes, flanked by various species of fish. A circle, divided by red tesserae into twelve panels, displayed the signs of the zodiac. Preserved (beginning at six o'clock and proceeding counterclockwise) are Capricorn, Aquarius, Pisces, Aries,

**7.22 Münster-Sarmsheim, sun-god mosaic**

Taurus, Gemini, Virgo, Libra, and Scorpio; Cancer, Leo, and Sagittarius are missing. The zodiac is the appropriate surround for the unique central medallion, which displays the sun-god, wearing a radiate crown and a streaming cloak, and carrying a whip, driving the four spirited horses of his chariot. In order to make the horses fit the circular space, the mosaicist has had to depict them rearing.

Nine miles south of Bingen, in Bad Kreuznach, in the attractive valley of the Nahe, lay a villa where in 1893/4 a particularly ornate mosaic, also of about the mid-third century A.D., was excavated. Damaged in World War II, it was carefully restored nine years later, in such a way as to distinguish properly between ancient and modern tesserae. It may be visited *in situ* in the Hüffelsheimerstrasse west of the town. We have had occasion to note before that mosaicists worked from pattern-books. This mosaic (Fig. 7.23) returns to a favorite motif: hunting and gladiatorial combat. In the central medallion, two hunters, one mounted, one on foot, attack a variety of animals. The immediate victim is a panther (with square spots!); below are a stag, a bull, and a boar, which have already been disposed of. There is also a bear with a spear broken off in his body, a spotted stag, a prancing wild goat with magnificent horns, and a highly indignant lion. Around the central medallion, in arched panels, are eight gladiatorial scenes, alternating contests between man and man and man and beast. Various types of gladiator are identifiable by their armor. At the bottom, the lightly armed *retiarius* (net-man) pitted against a *secutor*, with oblong shield; at the top, a pair of *murmillones*, with round shields; at the left, Thracians, one with a dagger, one with a spear; at the right, a Samnite with outstretched shield-arm, about to deal with his sword the deathblow to a wounded Thracian in visored helmet, who, having lost his shield and broken his sword, begs in vain for mercy. The other four panels pit a gladiator against wounded animals, rearing, or sitting back

7.23 Bad Kreuznach, gladiator-mosaic

on their haunches: a panther, a boar, a bear, and a bull. The bull has a spear sticking out between his shoulders in the mortal spot nowadays aimed at by Spanish bullfighters. In the corners, wild beasts attack their prey: bear and stag, leopard and boar, lion and bull, panther and wild ass.

As we contemplate these scenes of unrelieved sadism, it is at least pleasant to reflect that the Romans did not succeed in passing on to modern Germans their taste for these repellent scenes of wholesale carnage in the name of sport.

# 8 : *Afterglow*

E have seen repeatedly how much damage the invasions of the Alemanni did along the Limes and the Rhine in A.D. 260. One by-product was the rise within the provinces of Upper and Lower Germany and Belgica of warring pretenders to the throne. Among these Postumus (A.D. 258-268) and his Praetorian Prefect and successor Victorinus (268-270) used as their capital Trier (Augusta Treverorum), in the fertile Mosel valley, shut in by vine-clad hills. It had been founded by Augustus, made a colony by Claudius, and, before the barbarians came, had enjoyed the peace and prosperity evidenced by the villas in the Mosel valley nearby. When Diocletian stabilized the Empire in A.D. 293, and divided it into four great regions, he assigned Trier, as capital of the West, to his Caesar, Constantius Chlorus, the father of Constantine the Great. This was the beginning of the late bloom of the city and its fertile hinterland, which it will be the business of this chapter to describe.

There are more Roman monuments well-preserved above ground in Trier than in any other city in Germany. The plan (Fig. 8.1) shows the grid (reminiscent of Augst), which dates from Claudius' time, and the later Roman wall. We shall identify the numbered monuments, and then describe some of them in greater detail. At (1) on the plan is the north gate, the Porta Nigra; (2) is a double warehouse, discovered since World War II; (3) is the Cathedral, with two early churches under it; (4) is the

215

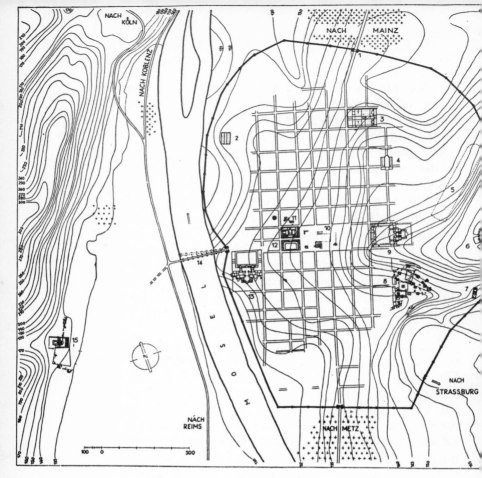

8.1 Trier, plan

very impressive so-called "Basilica," restored since the war, and in use as a Lutheran church; (5) is the probable site of the Circus; (6) the amphitheater, later incorporated into the walls, as at Avenches; (7) is a Roman temple at the Herrenbrünnchen; (8) is the Altbach Gallo-Roman sacred precinct, already described in Chapter 6; (9) is the Imperial Baths-Palace complex; (10) is the Forum; (11) is the palace of the pretender-Emperor Victorinus, identified from his name in a mosaic inscription; (12) is a palace complex; (13) is the Barbara Baths; and (14) shows the earlier (downstream) and later phases of the Roman bridge; (15) is the Lenus-Mars precinct, also already described and illustrated in Chapter 6.

The oldest surviving building in Trier is the amphitheater, a rebuilding in buttressed concrete and stone (about A.D. 100) of an earlier version in wood. With a capacity of 20,000, and an arena measuring 164 x 246 feet, it is the tenth largest of the seventy-two known in the Empire, about the same size as the one in Verona. The amphitheater in Trier is probably the setting of the gladiator-and-beast-fight mosaics in the villas at Nennig and Bad Kreuznach. The reconstruction-drawing (Fig. 8.2) shows how its right half was built into the hillside. Earth excavated for the arena was banked up on the left (west) side as underpinning for the seats there.

The amphitheater was sited at the end of Roman Trier's main east-west street, the Decumanus Maximus (see plan, Fig. 8.1). A tunnel running under the west seats gave access to the Imperial box. Two transverse gangways divided the amphitheater's seating into three sections, partly reserved, as inscriptions show. The lower tiers were considered the best, as in an American baseball park: here the notables sat in comfortable armchairs on a podium, protected from danger by the fact that the arena level was sunk ten feet below them. In the arena wall were the entrances to fourteen cages, for beasts or condemned criminals. In them were found curse-tablets scrawled by the wretches before the end; also a couple of ivory boxes with Christian symbols, reminding us that, as Saki rather un-

**8.2 Trier, amphitheater, reconstruction drawing**

feelingly puts it, the early Christian got the fattest lion. (The Christians had their revenge in the end: in 1211 the amphitheater was deeded to the monks of Himmerod for use as a stone quarry, which is why there is now so little of it left.) In the center of the arena was a cross-shaped excavation, in which iron and lead counterweights were found. This is what remains of the mechanism for raising to the arena level appropriate backdrops of desert or forest scenery for the beast-fights. The Coliseum in Rome shows the same arrangement.* When not in use, the space was covered with planking and sanded over. As the reconstruction-drawing shows, there were three entrances on the south (with a corresponding arrangement on the north). The central entrance communicated with the arena only; the lateral ones gave access to the lower tiers of seats. Access to the upper tier was by long, steep flights of stairs on either side of the ground-level entrance, leading to a terrace with frequent archways opening on the upper seats. This made arrival and departure easy for the 20,000 spectators. The façade was monumentally treated, like the Porta Nigra.

In the second century A.D., when Trier was provided with a circuit-wall, the amphitheater was incorporated into it, in such a way that the north entrance was within the wall, the south entrance outside it, so that the amphitheater formed an elaborate double gate (see plan, Fig. 8.1), and questionable persons could be halted and searched in the arena.

The Porta Nigra, the hundred-foot-high north gate in Trier's late-second-century wall, is the best-preserved Roman monument of German soil, and the best-preserved city gate anywhere in the Roman world. It owes this happy state to Christianity. In 1028, Simeon, a hermit from the East, came to Trier and applied for permission to be sealed up in the gate. He died there in 1035. When he was sancti-

---

* See *The Mute Stones Speak*, p. 235; paperback, p. 231.

fied in 1047, the archbishop converted the gate into St. Simeon's Church, removing the top story of the east tower, and converting the other into a belfry, but preserving the rest as the main body of the church. The apse is a twelfth-century addition, rather tastefully blended with the original architecture. Napoleon, having melted down the lead roof and the bronze doors for his own purposes, later ordered, and the Prussian government that followed his fall carried out, the clearing away of the medieval accretions, and the restoration of the gate to its present form (Fig. 8.3).

The Porta Nigra—so called from the black patina deposited on the red sandstone by weather and soot—was designed to be impressive, as a palatial façade, and practical, as a military barrier. Impressive it is, like the Tabularium in Rome,* with its massive blocks, put together without mortar, and its broad double entrance arches, each fifteen feet wide and twenty-three feet high, framed by half-columns, which are then repeated in the smaller arched windows on the stories above. On the practical side, its ground-floor has no windows, only archery slits, and its towers are rounded, to give a wider field of fire. It is seventy feet deep, for the double entrance opened into a court overlooked on all four sides, so as to keep questionable travelers covered. The side of the gate facing the enemy could be closed by a portcullis: the slots in which it rose and fell are visible. But on the side facing the town, projecting bosses would make it impossible to close the gate, and indeed at the time it was built (A.D. 166-200) there was no imperious military necessity. (The date has been deduced from over 200 masons' marks on the construction-blocks.)

At the same time as Trier's wall and the Porta Nigra, and at the opposite end of the Decumanus Maximus from the amphitheater, the Romans built a bridge with stone piers across the Mosel (Fig. 8.4, and plan, Fig. 8.1, 14).

* See *The Mute Stones Speak*, Fig. 5.9.

The approach to it from the town is by the Karl-Marx-strasse. It is amusing that this city, so bourgeois both in Roman times and in our own, should have been the birth-place of the father of Communism. In 1921 were dis-covered, just downstream from it, the wooden piers of an earlier bridge, in the middle of which, in A.D. 70, as Tacitus records in his *Histories*, the Roman general Cerialis, with-out his armor but with a small band of picked men, met and stopped the insurgent Treveri.

Five of the seven piers of the stone bridge are Roman. They were built of large blocks of blue-black basaltic lava, in the same technique as the Porta Nigra, that is, without mortar, being held together with iron clamps. To allow for flooding, there were two more piers on the east bank. On the upstream side, the piers are pointed, to serve as ice-breakers, and to meet the force of the current; on the downstream side they are curved. Visible in the photograph are the projecting stone consoles on which the wooden arches of the superstructure rested: the stone arches are medieval. Underwater, the archaeologists found the remains of the oak caissons within which the piers were built. The

8.3  Trier, Porta Nigra

8.4 Trier, Roman bridge

bridge carried the road from Gaul up to the city's east gate, now vanished, but once as impressive as the Porta Nigra. The city wall bent in at this point, in order to give the defenders of the gate flanking fire. Constantius Chlorus (Caesar A.D. 293-305) struck coins portraying the wall and bridge; they were minted here, in the capital of the West. The traveler from Gaul, reaching the city by this bridge, had an impressive view of the ornate east gate, the massive Barbara Baths beside it, and the double warehouse (Fig. 8.1,2), symbol of prosperity, by the river-harbor half a mile to the north downstream.

The traveler crossing the city from the bridge followed the Decumanus, passed the forum, and came, on his left, to the Imperial Baths, among the largest in the Empire (853 feet square), three-quarters the size of the Baths of Caracalla in Rome. They were built toward the end of the third century A.D. It has been calculated that to build them today would cost $40,000,000. In the Middle Ages, when godliness ranked ahead of cleanliness, the ruins of the enormous structure were incorporated into the reduced circuit of the city wall, and one of the huge arched windows did duty as a city gate. Modern excavation, as at the Saalburg, was encouraged by Kaiser Wilhelm II. The preliminary report was delivered to him on July 30, 1914. Within a month, he had other matters on his mind, and the baths were used as a prisoner-of-war camp for allied officers in World War I.

The photograph (Fig. 8.5), taken from the southeast, shows the massive superstructure of the caldarium (120 x 66 feet), the excavated ground-plan of other parts of the complex (round tepidarium, frigidarium with pools, sudatorium—originally vaulted—and dressing rooms) to the west. In the upper right quadrant is the Landesmuseum, crammed with rich finds from Trier and environs, and (top center) the so-called "Basilica," to be discussed below. As the photograph shows, the concrete walls were faced with limestone, with occasional courses of brick, a technique known to ancient masons as *opus listatum*. The bulk and impressiveness of the original building is best appreciated in the reconstruction-drawing (Fig. 8.6). This shows, besides the main building, with its apse housing one of the frigidarium pools, the vast porticoed exercise-ground (308 x 223 feet), and the arcaded façade with the entrance treated like a monumental arch. Below ground the baths were honeycombed with a labyrinth of tunnels, in two stories, great fun to explore. The upper story was intended for the use of service personnel, especially in supplying wood to the furnaces; the lower contained the drains. The baths received their water supply from their own aqueduct. Marble veneer (*opus sectile*) and frescoes embellished the walls; there were many mosaics.

But this grandiose pile was never finished, nor even, apparently, used. In the 360s the Emperor Valentinian I (reigned A.D. 364-375) remodeled the baths into a palace, transforming the caldarium into a basilica, blocking the tunnels, and constructing a scruffy set of small baths northeast of the caldarium. Excavation in the 1960s revealed that the western section, under the exercise-ground, had been thickly and prosperously settled between the first and the third centuries A.D. The houses had wall paintings of aquatic scenes, and there was a huge mosaic, eighty-five

8.5  Trier, Imperial Baths, photograph

8.6  Trier, Imperial Baths, reconstruction drawing

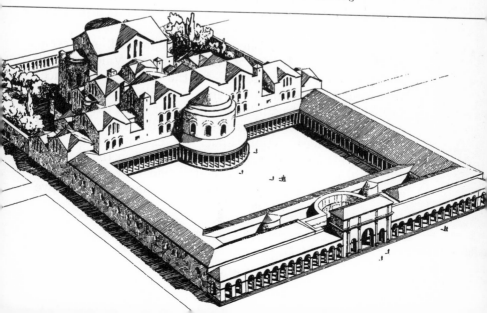

8.7 Trier, Polydus mosaic

feet square, the central octagon of which (Fig. 8.7) portrayed a charioteer in a four-horse chariot. He has a Greek name, Polydus, wears the standard charioteer's corselet of leather thongs, and proudly brandishes his whip, together with the palm and wreath of victory.

North of the baths lies the "Basilica," now splendidly but simply restored as a Lutheran church, after serious World War II damage. It was built about A.D. 310 as the throne-room of Constantine's palace. Since then, it has been the residence of Frankish kings, archbishops, and Counts Palatine; a pesthouse, and a barracks. It was first converted into a Protestant church by King Friedrich Wilhelm of Prussia between 1846 and 1856. It is, after the Pantheon in Rome, the largest surviving building of the Roman world: 250 feet long, 90 feet wide, and 98 feet high (see model, Fig. 8.8). Its brick-faced concrete walls, which in antiquity were stuccoed, and painted between the windows with yellow flowers on a red ground, are nearly nine feet thick; their footings go down thirteen to twenty feet. In antiquity the soaring effect of its high, slim arches—nine on the long sides, four in the apse—was broken by two balconies, reached from the interior by winding stairs at either side of the apse. From the balconies, it was possible to open, shut, clean, and repair the windows; the balconies also served to mask the outlet ducts for the tubes that heated the walls.

**8.8 Trier, "Basilica," model**

**8.9 Trier, "Basilica," reconstruction drawing**

As the model shows, the "Basilica" did not originally stand isolated, as today. Recent excavation has shown that it stood in a porticoed courtyard, with another courtyard to the east, and a vestibule (narthex) in front, which opened on yet another porticoed court. The effect is best seen in the reconstruction-drawing, Figure 8.9. Cryptoporticoes, still accessible, ran under the porticoes of the south courtyard. The effect must have been very like that of the procurator's palace already described in Köln, and indeed in Trier the same excavations that revealed the courtyards struck, on a lower level, the remains of the palace of the procurator of the province of Belgica; this preceded the present complex. Constantine's throne-room, then, represented a new departure only in its colossal size. It was simply the major building in a traditional plan, built where Trier's administrative center had been since the time of Augustus.

The interior, as now restored, is stuccoed gray, exquisitely restrained and unadorned. Such was not the effect for which Constantine's interior decorators strove. Their aim was to dazzle. The radiant-heated floors were paved in black and white marble (*opus sectile*), the walls were encrusted with polychrome marble, and the apse, where the throne stood, gleamed with a mosaic of blue-green garlands on a gold ground. The awestruck visitor, admitted to audience of the Emperor, not only had to traverse the 275-foot stretch from narthex-entrance to the throne, but found the distance seemingly increased by a trick of perspective, brought about by setting the apse windows deep, and reducing their size as compared with the side windows, so that they seemed much farther away than they actually were. Constantine was an absolute monarch, who expected his subjects to prostrate themselves before him. In the Trier throne-room, his architect contrived by his effects that they should be induced to do so.

Not far west of the "Basilica," excavation for a new building in 1950 laid bare a most unusual mosaic (Fig. 8.10). The large scene at the top gives the clue. It represents the birth from an egg (on an altar) of Helen, who was to grow up to be the most beautiful woman in the world, and her brothers, Castor and Pollux. The birth from an egg is logical, since their mother Leda (also represented) was seduced by Zeus in the form a swan. Zeus (here "Iobis") is here symbolized as an eagle. Agamemnon, also present, is an interested party: he was Leda's son-in-law, having married her daughter Clytemnestra, and Helen was to deceive his brother Menelaus, run off with Trojan Paris, and provoke Agamemnon to lead the Greeks against Troy. The other large panel below is a scene of sacrifice. This is the mosaic floor of the chapel of a cult, hitherto unknown, of Leda's children. The mosaic was laid in the late fourth century, in the reign of Valentinian or Gratian (A.D. 375-383). By that time Christianity had a firm foothold in Trier, and, oddly enough, the performer of the sacrifice has a Christian name, Quodvul[t] deus ("What-God-Wills"), which curiously anticipates English Puritan names like Praise-God Barebones. Apparently Christians did not regard this cult and their own as mutually exclusive. In the round medallions, six named local worthies carry trays of food on their heads; in the ovals are men busy with drink, lamp, and incense; and two dancing girls.

8.11 Trier, double warehouse, model

The Emperor controlled commerce as well as politics, and with equal elegance. The archaeological evidence is the previously mentioned double warehouse (Fig. 8.11), for food, arms, and equipment, a wall of which was laid bare by bombing in World War II, and has been preserved in rebuilding St. Irminien. The complex is as long as the "Basilica," and twice as wide, the two buildings being separated by a wagon road giving access to both. The walls combine limestone and brick, as in the Imperial Baths, and the outer treatment with two stories of blind arcades suggests the same architectural tradition as the "Basilica." The suggested date, however, is somewhat later, in the reign of Valentinian I.

The citizens of Trier who turned thumbs down on the gladiators in the amphitheater, passed back and forth through the Porta Nigra or across the bridge, spent their leisure in the baths, did obeisance before the Emperor's throne, and derived their livelihood from the contents of the warehouses were obviously prosperous. They were, as we shall see, proud of the sources of their wealth. They were also eager to prove how completely they had assimilated Graeco-Roman culture. The evidence for this eagerness is to be seen in the many mosaics: two-thirds of all the Roman mosaics known from Germany have been found in or near Trier, and most of them, including the ones illustrated here, were ordered from pattern-books reflecting

8.10 Trier, Leda-cult mosaic

**229**

the taste of the metropolis, not the indigenous cultural roots of the province.

The style of the mosaics, now on display in the Landesmuseum, dates them mostly between A.D. 200 and 250. Figure 8.12, found in 1898 in the Johannisstrasse, behind Karl Marx' birthplace, shows the pre-Socratic philosopher Anaximander illustrating how a sundial works. Figure 8.13, found in the Neustrasse, near the forum, in 1942, depicts in nine panels the nine Muses. Only the ones with attributes can be identified. The one with the mask in the upper left-hand corner is Thalia, muse of comedy. Next to

**8.12 Trier, Anaximander mosaic**

8.13 Trier, Muses mosaic

8.14 Trier, Dionysus mosaic

her, with a lyre, is Terpsichore, muse of the dance, and next to her, with a scroll, is Clio, muse of history. Under her is Erato, muse of love-poetry, and in the lower left panel, with a celestial globe, is Urania, muse of astronomy. The Dionysus-mosaic, found in 1902 in the Walramsneustrasse, came from the same pattern-book as the mosaic previously described in Köln. The central medallion (Fig. 8.14) shows the wine-god and a satyr, with a span of panthers. The ovals portray the seasons, and in the trapezoids are wagons drawn by boars, panthers, lions, and stags. The most amusing mosaic (Fig. 8.15), found in the Sudallee, near the Forum, in 1875, shows a greedy bear gaping

**8.15 Trier, bear mosaic**

up a tree after fruit. The most elaborate of the series (Fig. 8.16) is signed by the mosaicist, whose name was Monnus. It has fifty-three panels. In the octagons, Muses instruct wise men. In the squares are Latin and Greek authors: the historian Livy, the orator Cicero, the epic poet Ennius, the comic poet Menander; and two poets who told the story of farming, which made Trier rich: the Greek Hesiod and the Roman Vergil. In the corners are the seasons, and in the trapezoids the signs of the zodiac. Twelve squares represent the gods who preside over the months.

Trier was the market town for the prosperous vineyard owners who lived in the Mosel valley. In 1878, in the walls of a Constantinian fort at Neumagen, twenty-five miles down-river from Trier, was found a famous series of reliefs, now in the Trier museum, which might serve to illustrate Ausonius' poem about the Mosel. The visitors' favorite is the "Happy Steersman" (Fig. 8.17), the pilot of a wine-barge, pillowing his head on a wine-barrel from which he has obviously drunk deep and with pleasure. One can imagine him calling to the vinedressers on the bank, as Ausonius describes (*Mosella*, 163-168):

( A folk rejoicing in labor, husbandmen busy and nimble
Move and work on the heights and along the slopes of the valley,
Singing their country ditties. To some the traveler journeying
Under the bank responds, and some from his vessel the sailor
Mocks in answering song because they are late to the vineyards.
Echoes ring from the rocks and the shore and the trembling forests.

**8.16 Trier, Monnus mosaic**

8.18 Neumagen, tenants paying rent, relief

These reliefs, though of the same date as the Trier mosaics, breathe a very different spirit. They are of the earth earthy: they pay no lip service to imported culture, but reflect, with the humor, realism, and individuality of good snapshots, everyday life in the Mosel villas. Figure 8.18, for example, shows the tenants paying their rent. The tenants are bearded, the owner's clerks clean-shaven. At the left, a farmer with his forefinger raised in dispute is arguing over the amount he should pay; before him lie the account book and a scratch tablet, with a basketful of money beside them. Behind the table in the center a pair of clerks and a tenant are haggling over a heap of money. The clerk is suggesting that a coin he holds in his right hand is counterfeit; of this notion the bearded farmer is obviously taking a dim view. Meanwhile the other clerk is counting the take. The farmer at the right holds a purse, the contents of which he is about, reluctantly, to pay over.

Other reliefs show the owner and his family in homely situations. In Figure 8.19 the mistress of the house, wearing a combing-jacket, and seated in a basket-chair, her sandaled feet on a footstool, is having her hair washed and set, with the assistance of four maids. One is finishing the hair-

8.17 Neumagen, Jolly Steersman, relief

237

8.19  Neumagen, hairdressing scene, relief

8.20  Neumagen, schoolroom scene, relief

dressing, the second holds a bottle of hair oil in the crook of her arm, the third offers a mirror in which her mistress may admire the result, and the fourth, her labors finished, holds a water jug. Another relief (Fig. 8.20) shows the junior members of the family in the schoolroom. The bearded tutor is presiding over a reading lesson. His pupils, seated comfortably, like their instructor, in cane chairs, are reciting from scrolls. The ten-o'clock scholar on the right, who is late, is either apologizing for being tardy, or giving one of his classmates the right answer.

At Igel, on the Roman highway between Trier and Reims, stands what may well be the most interesting archaeological document of Roman Germany: the seventy-five-foot red sandstone grave-monument (Fig. 8.21) of a family of rich cloth merchants, the Secundini, who flourished at the same time as the nabobs who commissioned the Neumagen reliefs. A replica stands conveniently in the court of the Trier Landesmuseum. The monument combines scenes from Graeco-Roman myths of immortality with vignettes of daily life. Goethe compared its shape and symbolic effect to a lighthouse. At the very top Jupiter's eagle carries off Ganymede to be cupbearer in heaven; this relief is perched on a pine cone. Next below is the pyramidal crown of the monument, treated in a scale pattern. In the pediments are the sun and moon; the Greek myth of the youth Hylas, carried off by nymphs enamored of his beauty; and the Roman legend of Mars and Rhea Silvia, the mother of the twins Romulus and Remus, founders of Rome. The rectangular panels below show scenes in the cloth shop and the countingroom; a Genius flanked by griffins; and a two-mule gig, driver (with whip), and passenger, on the way to Trier (Fig. 8.22). A milestone in the background is marked L. IIII, or four leagues, which

is just the distance from Igel to Trier. Milestones in this area began to be marked in leagues instead of Roman miles in the reign of Septimius Severus (A.D. 193-211); this helps to date the monument. Further scenes from daily life enliven the long narrow panels below the cornice (Figs. 8.23a, b). On the front face is the family kitchen. At the left a servant brings a plate from the dining room. Next is a man at a table with his sleeves rolled up, working with a knife. The platters that seem to be hanging are intended to be thought of as on the table: the artist in his primitive way has simply set them up on edge to give a better view. Under the table is a tub and a water bucket. The scullion in the center is washing a bowl; at the far right the chef is preparing a dish at the stove for the servant, who waits, a napkin over his shoulder. On the west face, tenants bring gifts in kind to their landlord, who stands before a curtain at the right; the gifts are a hare, a fish, a lamb, a fur or skin, a chicken, and something in a bucket; the family conversing at a meal; and two pack animals, loaded with bales of cloth, crossing a mountain (Fig. 8.24).

The main relief, framed by pilasters, shows the Secundini brothers, their will, and their heir, a boy; a woman and two children are in the medallions above, and an inscription below records their names. The monument owes its preservation to the pious belief that these figures represented Constantine's father, Constantius Chlorus, and his mother, St. Helena, together with Constantine himself. The scenes on the other faces of the monument at this level are mythological, expressing the hope of immortality: the apotheosis of Hercules, with Perseus rescuing Andromeda from the sea monster; the Isles of the Blest, with Achilles' mother, Thetis, dipping him in the Styx to make him invulnerable; and the realm of Dionysus. Below the inscriptions are more scenes of daily life: a scroll being

8.21 Igel, grave-monument of Secundini

**8.22 Igel, gig on way to Trier, relief**

**8.23a, b Igel, kitchen scene; tenants bringing gifts, relief**

read; rolls and bales of cloth; and (Fig. 8.25) a four-wheeled wagon, loaded with corded bales, drawn by three mules, and emerging from an arched gate that looks like the one in Figure 8.22: the product of the factory being driven to market in Trier. The gate no doubt belongs to the Secundini's *villa rustica*, which has never been located, but may well be under the Igel village church, visible in the background of Figure 8.21. On the steps of the monument are conventional motifs alluding probably to traffic on the Mosel: Cupids with dolphins, ships loaded with bales, being towed; and Tritons. There are no dolphins in the Mosel, but there are no Cupids or Tritons in it either; no doubt the Secundini brothers found it all very elegant. And indeed there breathes from the monument the harmless vanity of successful businessmen, proving that they have made good, and using their tombstone to attest to their solvency. We should be grateful to the Secundini for these snapshots of their prosperity. These scenes make the villas and the warehouses come to life, and would make excellent illustrations for Ausonius' poem, written some four generations later, when Trier and the Mosel valley were enjoying their afterglow.

Ausonius knew well the Imperial summer palace at Konz (Contionacum), in a stunning location on the high promontory where the Saar joins the Mosel, opposite Igel (Fig. 8.26). Its plan is like that of the "Basilica" complex in Trier on a smaller scale (275 x 125 feet): a lofty, radiant-heated throne-room with arched windows in the center, and porticoed courtyards on either side; the Imperial private apartments open off. It too was built for Constantine, and continued in use down to the time of Valentinian I, whose successor Gratian, we remember, Ausonius tutored before he came to the throne. The shady porticoes on the cool north side, high over the river, afforded an enchanting

8.24 Igel, pack-animals crossing mountain, relief

view. The Emperor had extensive and elegant private baths
in the west wing. The exterior walls, thick for coolness,
were stuccoed and painted, with motifs in yellow and green,
and red garlands on a white ground. Here indeed was an
idyllic spot in which to enjoy the afterglow of Imperial
splendor. Only forty years after Ausonius enjoyed the hospitality of this spacious, elegant, and charming palace, the
barbarian was hammering at the gates of Rome itself. No
doubt the Empire would have lasted longer if the Emperors
had attended more to the defense of the realm and the
welfare of their subjects. But, in a time of the breaking of
nations, there is something to be said for elegance, too,
and in the long run this turned out to be one of Rome's
most durable gifts to her German provinces.

A good deal of controversy rages in Germany about the
degree of cultural continuity between Roman times and
the Middle Ages. Some nationalists deny it, but no student
of archaeology can entirely share their view. This book has
cited a number of examples that tend to show that the
continuity is real: the seed of the Middle Ages was sown
in Germany in late Roman times. To recognize this need
deal no blow to German national pride: the deeper the
roots, the more cause for self-congratulation. The emerging German states of the Middle Ages owed their existence
to merchants' guilds, which prospered on continuing long-
distance trade, a heritage from Rome, as we have seen.
One scholar aptly compares Germany's Roman heritage
to a ruined garden: some plants die, but some survive,

**244**

taking a longer or a shorter time to bloom again. And when they do, they are reminiscent of Rome, and reminders of a fact that modern nations would do well to remember, that there is a future in tradition, and that the past is never dead.

In this book we have seen how Rome brought to the noble savages romanticized by Tacitus some of the blessings—and some of the bane, such as taxation, a military establishment, and absolutism—of what Mediterranean man understood by civilization, and how its subjects contrived to impress what they borrowed with their own distinctive German stamp.

It is not such a far cry after all from the crude power of the Gundestrup cauldron, with its motifs from a fierce native religion, to the primitive representation in the Trier mosaic of Leda's children born from an egg. Seven centuries and more before Constantine built his summer palace at

**8.25 Igel, wagon with bales of cloth, relief**

8.26 Konz, Constantine's summer palace, reconstruction drawing

Konz, an anonymous German prince built his at the Heuneburg on the Danube, and the architecture of both has Greek roots. When Caesar threw his bridge across the Rhine, he linked German culture with Rome forever. We have seen the evidence in the cities, replicas of planned Italian towns: Nyon, Augst and Köln; Windisch, Kempten, and Augsburg; Bonn, Strassburg, and Trier.

We have seen how Arminius forced the Romans to draw in their horns, and how for decades the Limes drew the line between barbarism and civilization, enabling Germans and Romans alike to lead the good life behind the protection of its wall, in spas like Badenweiler, Wiesbaden, and Baden-Baden; in villas enriching the landscape in Switzerland and Austria, as well as in Baden-Württemberg, the Eifel, and the lovely Mosel valley.

We have seen how soldiers and traders brought to Germany the sometimes weird consolations of exotic religions, without stamping out what was native. We have been impressed by Roman tolerance of subjects who behaved: beside the temples of official cult, the German worship of the hammer-god, and the Celtic rites of Rosmerta, Lenus-Mars, Epona, and the Matronae with their beehive headdresses. And we have looked at the memorials of gods from Syria, Asia Minor, Egypt, and Persia, and recognized Christianity, as the Germans did, as yet another, more comforting faith brought from the East.

We have seen how inventively the Germans adopted Graeco-Roman techniques, in architecture, sculpture in stone and bronze, pottery, hydraulics, surgery, viticulture, glass, and mosaic.

The result of four centuries of Roman occupation was to link the West of Germany forever with the older cultures of the south. This is a history of which, on balance, any people might well be proud, and it augurs well for the unity of Europe that German archaeologists, to whose labors in field and study this book owes so much, are making their countrymen ever more aware of the existence, the strength, and the enduring power of that link. Germans under Roman sway gained, on the whole, more than they lost, and most modern Germans would agree that it was a boon for their fatherland to have had the Romans on the Rhine.

# ACKNOWLEDGMENTS

Amsterdam: Instituut voor Prae–en Protohistorie: 3.27
Augst, Römerhaus: 2.6–8, 10
Avenches, Musée Romain: 3.28; 6.14; 7.9–10
Basel:
R. Laur-Belart: 2.3; 5.5, 6
Benno Schwabe: 5.7
Schweizerische Reederei AG: 2.11
Berlin, Gebrüder Mann: 1.9, 11; 7.19
Bern, Historisches Museum: 2.4, 5; 6.13
Biel, Museum Schwab: 7.15
Bingen, Heimatmuseum der Kreisstadt: 7.18
Brugg, Vindonissa Museum: 3.16–18
Bonn, Rheinisches Landesmuseum: 1.8; 2.1; 3.3–5; 7.14, 23; 5.11, 12; 6.9, 12; 7.4, 12, 22
Budapest, Akademiai Kiadó: 5.10
Copenhagen, Danish National Museum: 1.1, 3.7
Darmstadt, Hessisches Landesmuseum: 7.11
Dieburg, Kreis- und Stadtmuseum: 6.18, 19
Duisburg, DEMAG: 7.1
Düsseldorf, Econ Verlag: 3.25
Engelskirchen, Verlag H. Steube: 4.4, 6–8
Frankfurt, Römisch-Germanische Kommission: 4.1, 15
Freudenstadt, Muller Fotokarten: 5.4
Haltern, Römisch-Germanisches Museum: 7.13
Heidelberg, C. Winter Universitätsverlag: 1.4
Kempten, Museum: 3.20
Köln, Römisch-Germanisches Museum: 2.12, 13, 15–19, 21; 7.3, 20, 21
Stadtmuseum: 2.14
Leyden, Museum: 7.5
Madison, Wisconsin, University of Wisconsin Cartographic Lab.: 1, 2; 3.1, 2; 5.1; 6.1
Mainz: Mittelrheinisches Landesmuseum: 3.9, 12; 6.6; 7.2
Römisch-Germanisches Zentralmuseum: 2.2; 3.6, 8, 10; 4.12; 5.3; 6.3
Mannheim, Verlag E. Hartmann: 4.5
Munich, Deutscher Kunstverlag: 3.21; 4.16
Bayer. Landesamt für Denkmalpflege: 1.12–14; 4.11, 18–20

**249**

Neuss, Clemens-Sels-Museum: 3.22
Princeton, New Jersey, Alison Frantz: 7.7
Regensburg, Museum der Stadt: 6.17; 7.6
Rome, Fototeca: 7.16
Saalburg, Museum: 4.2, 3, 9, 21
Saarbrücken, Landesmuseum: 6.2
Scherndorf, Strähle: 4.14
Schleswig, Landesmuseum: 1.5, 6
Speyer, Historisches Museum: 6.20; 7.8
Stuttgart, Württembergisches Landesmuseum: 1, 10; 6.4, 8
Trier, Rheinisches Landesmuseum: 3.15; 5.2, 13–18; 6.5, 7, 10, 15; 7.17–23; 8.1–26
Utrecht, Provinciaal Oudheidkundig Museum: 7.14
Vienna, Österreichisches arch. Inst.: 3.24; 5.8, 9
Wiesbaden, Städtisches Museum: 6.16
Worms, Museum der Stadt: 6.11
Zürich, Swissair: 2.9
 W. Drack: 2.3

All other photographs are by the author

# BOOKS AND ARTICLES CONSULTED

*Abbreviations*

BRGK: *Berichte der Römisch-Germanischen Kommission*
BJ: *Bonner Jahrbücher*
CAH: *Cambridge Ancient History*
Doppelfeld, 1967a: O. Doppelfeld, ed., *Römer am Rhein:* (Köln 1967)
G: *Germania*
GR²: *Germania Romana*, 2nd ed., parts 4-5, ed. F. Koepp, G. Bersu (Bamberg 1928-30)
*Gymn.*: *Gymnasium*
NAD: *Neue Ausgrabungen in Deutschland* (Berlin 1958)
Pörtner²: R. Pörtner, *Mit dem Fahrstuhl in die Römerzeit*, 2nd ed. (Munich-Zurich 1967)
RE: *Pauly's Realencyclopädie der classischen Altertumswissenschaft*
RGF: *Römisch-Germanische Forschungen*


1: *Before the Romans*

K. Bittel, A. Rieth, *Heuneburg* (Stuttgart 1951)
O. Brogan, *Roman Gaul* (London 1953)
W. Dehn, "Die Heuneburg an der oberen Donau und ihre Wehranlagen," NAD 127-145
J. Filip, *Die keltische Zivilisation und ihr Erbe* (Prague 1961)
A. Grenier, *Les Gaulois* (Paris 1945)
W. Haarnagel, "Die Ergebnisse der Grabung auf der Wurt Feddersen Wierde bei Bremerhaven in den Jahren von 1955-1957," NAD 215-228
P. Jacobsthal, *Early Celtic Art* (Oxford 1944)
J. Keller, "Das keltische Fürstengrab von Reinheim," NAD 146-160
W. Kimmig, *Die Heuneburg an der oberen Donau* (Stuttgart-Tübingen 1968)
———, E. Gersbach, "Die neuen Ausgrabungen auf der Heuneburg," G 44 (1966) 102-136
H. Last, "The Wars of the Age of Marius," CAH 9 (1932) 140-151
R. Much, *Die Germania des Tacitus³*, ed. H. Jankuhn, W. Lange (Heidelberg 1967)

E. Norden, *Alt-Germanien* (Leipzig 1934)
R. Pörtner, *Bevor die Römer kamen* (Düsseldorf-Vienna 1961)
T.G.E. Powell, *The Celts* (London 1958)
J. Roeder, "Der Goloring," *BJ* 148 (1948) 81-132
M. Schröder, R. Roeren, *Kleine Vor- und Frühgeschichte Württembergs* (Stuttgart 1963)

## 2: A Bridge and Three Colonies

D. van Berchem, "Zur römischen Kolonisation in der Schweiz," *Jahrbuch der schweizerischer Gesellschaft für Urgeschichte* 46 (1957) 13-23
O. Doppelfeld, "Die römische Stadtmauer von Köln," *Kölner Untersuchungen*, Beiheft 2 (1950) 1-40
————, ed., *Ausgewählte Quellen zur Kölner Stadtgeschichte* 1 (Köln 1958)
————, 1967a
————, "Das Dionysus-Mosaik am Dom zu Köln," *Schriftenreihe der archäologischen Gesellschaft Köln* 8[3] (1967)
W. Drack, ed., *Repertorium der Ur- und Frühgeschichte der Schweiz* 4 (Basel 1958)
F. Fremersdorf, "Der römische Gutshof Köln-Müngersdorf," *RGF* 6 (1933)
————, *Das Römergrab in Weiden bei Köln* (Köln 1957)
P. La Baume, *Colonia Agrippinensis*[3] (Köln 1964)
R. Laur-Belart, *Führer durch Augusta Raurica*[4] (Basel 1966)
K. Parlasca, *Die römische Mosaiken in Deutschland* (Berlin 1959)
H. von Petrikovits, "Das römische Rheinland: archäologische Forschungen seit 1945," *Arbeitsgemeinschaft für Forschung des Landes Nordrhein-Westfalen, Geisteswissenschaften* 86 (1960)
Pörtner[2]
K. Saatmann, E. Jüngst, P. Thielscher, "Caesars Rheinbrücke," *BJ* 143/4 (1938/9) 83-208
E. Samesreuther, "Römische Wasserleitungen in den Rheinlanden," *BRGK* 26 (1936) 24-157
F. Stähelin, *Die Schweiz in römischer Zeit*[3] (Basel 1947)

## 3: Imperialism, Disaster Retrenchment (13 B.C.-A.D. 73)

C. Albrecht, *Das Römerlager von Oberaden* 1 (Dortmund 1938)
D. Baatz, "Die Topographie des römischen Mainz," *Gymn.* Beiheft 1 (1960) 51-58

# Books and Articles Consulted

————, "Moguntiacum" *Limesforschungen* 4 (Berlin 1962)
M. Bersu, "Kunstgewerbe und Handwerk," GR
Doppelfeld, 1967a
H. Dragendorff, F. Koepp, E. Krüger, C. Schuchhardt, "Ausgrabungen bei Haltern," *Mitteilungen der Altertumskommission für Westfalen* 4 (1905) 1-29; 5 (1909) 1-85; 6 (1912) 1-32; 7 (1923) 1-10
A. E. van Giffen, "De romeinse castella in de dorpsheuvel te Valkenburg an de Rijn," *Jaarsverslag van de Vereeniging voor Terpenonderzoek* 33-37 (1948-53)
J.-J. Hatt, *Strasbourg au temps des Romains* (Strasbourg 1953)
H. Hinz, "Xanten zur Römerzeit," *Beiträge zur Geschichte und Volkskunde des Kreises Dinslaken am Niederrhein*, Beiheft 1 (Xanten 1967)
————, "Bericht über die Ausgrabungen in der Colonia Ulpia Traiana bei Xanten," *BJ* 167 (1967)
W. John, "Quinctilius (20)" *RE* (1963) Sp. 907-984
J. B. Keune, "Haltern," *RE* Supplementband 3 (1918) Sp. 883-884
W. Kleise, "Die öffentliche Bauten von Cambodunum: Baubeschreibung und Reconstruction," *Materialheften zur bayerischen Vorgeschichte* 18 (1962)
F. Koepp, GR
E. Kornemann, "Die erste Befreiungstat des deutschen Volkes (Varusschlacht)," *Erbe der Alten*, 2e Reihe (Leipzig 1934)
W. Krämer, "Cambodunum-Forschungen I: 1953," *Materialheften zur bay. Vorg.* 9 (1957) 117ff
R. Laur-Belart, *Vindonissa: kleiner Führer*[3] (Brugg 1964)
T. F. Meysels, *Auf Römerstrassen durch Österreich* (Vienna 1960)
A. Obermayr, *Römerstadt Carnuntum: Ruinen, Grabungen, Funde* (Vienna-Munich 1967)
E. Pernice, F. Winter, *Der Hildesheimer Silberfund* (Berlin 1901)
H. von Petrikovits, "Vetera," *RE* (1958) Sp. 1801-34
————, "Mogontiacum: Das römische Mainz," *Mainzer Zeitschrift* 58 (1963) 27ff.
————, *Novaesium: Das römische Neuss* (Köln-Graz 1957)
Pörtner[2]
E. Ritterling, "Das frührömische Lager bei Hofheim in Taunus," *Annalen des Vereins für Nassauische Altertumskunde* 40 (1912), 2 vols.
E. Sadée, *Das römische Bonn* (Bonn 1925)
W. Schleiermacher, "Augusta Vindelicum," *Gymn.* Beih. 1 (1960) 78-79
A. Schober, *Die Römerzeit in Österreich*[2] (Vienna 1955)

F. Stähelin, *Die Schweiz in römischer Zeit*[3] (Basel 1947)

A. Stieren, "Die römischen Lager bei Haltern in Westfalen," *Neue Deutsche Ausgrabungen* (Münster 1930) 190-198

E. Swoboda, "Carnuntum: seine Geschichte und seine Denkmäler[4]," *Römische Forschungen in Niederösterreich* 1[4] (Graz-Köln 1964)

R. Syme, "The Northern Frontiers under Augustus," *CAH* 10 (1934) 358-363, 373-381

E. Virieux, *Avenches, cité romaine* (Neuchâtel 1959)

### 4: The Wide Frontier

D. Baatz, "Wandmalereien aus einem Limeskastell," *Gymn.* 75 (1958) 262-269

————, H. Riediger, *Römer und Germanen am Limes* (Frankfurt a/M 1966)

————, *Die Saalburg: ein Führer durch das römische Kastell und seine Geschichte* (Bad Homburg 1968)

O. Brogan, "The Roman Limes in Germany," *Archaeological Journal* 92 (1935) 1-41

E. Fabricius, F. Hettner, O. von Sarwey, *Der Obergermanisch-Raetische Limes des Römerreiches*, 14 vols. (Berlin-Leipzig 1894-1937)

E. Fabricius, "Limes," *RE* (1926) Sp. 572-671

B. Heukemes, "Lopodunum-Ladenburg am Neckar," *Badische Fundberichte*, Sonderheft 1 (Karlsruhe-Freiburg 1962)

H.-J. Hundt, U. Fischer, "Die Grabungen in der Altstadt von Frankfurt-am-Main," *NAD* 391-408

L. Jacobi, *Das Römerkastell Saalburg*, 2 vols. (Bad Homburg 1897)

H. S. Jones, *Companion to Roman History* (Oxford 1913) 243-257

J. Keim, H. Klumbach, "Der römische Schatzfund von Straubing," *Münchener Beiträge zur Vor- und Frühgeschichte* 3 (1951)

H.-J. Kellner, "Ein Schatzfund aus dem Kastell Stockstadt," *G* 41 (1963) 119-122

Meysels, *op. cit.* in ch. 3

F. Ostwald, *Index of Potter's Stamps* (E. Bridgford 1931)

O. Paret, *Württemberg in Vor- und Frühgeschichtlicher Zeit* (Stuttgart 1961)

W. Schleiermacher, *Der römische Limes in Deutschland*[2] (Berlin 1961)

————, "Municipium Arae Flaviae," *Gymn.* Beih. 1 (1960) 59-63

H. Schönberger, "Neuere Grabungen am obergermanischen und rätischen Limes," *Limesforschungen* 2 (1962) 69-137

# Books and Articles Consulted

G. Ulbert, "Das römische Regensburg," *Gymn*. Beih. 1 (1960) 64-77

## 5: The Good Life

M. Barbey, *Urba: mosaiques et vestiges romains de Boscéaz près Orbe* (Orbe 1929)

Doppelfeld, 1967a

F. Drexel, "Die bürgerlichen Siedlungen," *GR* 2 (Bamberg 1924)

J. Helm, *Das römische Kurbad zu Badenweiler* (Badenweiler 1962)

C. Hosius, ed., *Ausonius, Mosella*[3] (Marburg 1926)

H. S. Jones, *op. cit.* in ch. 4, 170-184

G. Kropatschek, "Das römische Landhaus in Deutschland," *BRGK* 6 (1910/11) 51-78

R. Laur-Belart, "Der römische Gutshof von Ober-Entfelden im Aargau," *Ur-Schweiz* 16 (1952) 9-18

————, Th. Strübin, "Die römische Villa von Munzach bei Liestal," *ib.* 17 (1953) 1-14

H. Mylius, "Die römische Heilthermen von Badenweiler," *RGF* 12 (1936)

F. Oertel, "Die römische Villa bei Blankenheim in der Eifel," *BJ* 123 (1916) 210-225

O. Paret, "Baden-Baden," *Handbuch der historischen Stätten Deutschlands* (Stuttgart 1965)

Pörtner[2]

W. Schmid, "Siedlung und Gräberfeld von Chatissa-Katsch in Obersteiermark," *Jahreshefte des Österreichischen arch. Inst.* 25 (1929) 98-148

R. Schindler, *Das römische Mosaik von Nennig*, Saarbrücken, n.d.

H. Schoppa, "Die römische Kaiserzeit," *Schriften des städtischen Museums Wiesbaden* 6[2] (Wiesbaden 1967)

P. Steiner, *Römische Landhäuser im Trierer Bezirk* (Berlin 1923)

J. Steinhauser, "Die Langmauer bei Trier und ihr Bezirk," *Trierer Zeitschrift* (1931) 41-79

K. M. Swoboda, *Römische und romanische Paläste*[2] (Vienna 1924)

E. B. Thomas, *Römische Villen in Pannonien* (Budapest 1964) 177-192

Varro, *de re rustica*, tr. W.D. Hooper, H.B. Ash (Cambridge, Mass. 1934) 1.11-16

Vitruvius, *de architectura*, tr. F. Granger (ib.) 7.1

E. Wagner, *Fundstätten und Funde in Baden*, 2 vols. (Tübingen 1908-12)

ROMANS ON THE RHINE

## 6: *Other Gods than Ours*

F. Behn, "Das Mithrasheiligtum von Dieburg," *RGF* 1 (Berlin-Leipzig 1928)
O. Brogan, *op. cit.* in ch. 4
Doppelfeld 1967a
F. Fremersdorf, "Ergebnisse der Forschungen bei der St. Severinskirche in Köln," *NAD* 329-339
E. Gose et al., *Tempelbezirk im Altbachtale zu Trier* (Trier 1938)
———, *Der Tempelbezirk des Lenus-Mars in Trier* (Berlin 1955)
K. Helm, *Altgermanische Religionsgeschichte* 1 (Heidelberg 1913)
F. Koepp, *GR*
H. Lehner, "Der Tempelbezirk der Matronae Vacallinehae bei Pesch," *BJ* 125 (1919) 74-162
H. Menzel, *Die römischen Bronzen aus Deutschland* 2: *Trier* (Mainz 1966)
G. Rissow, "Götter und Kulte in der Rheinlanden," Doppelfeld 1967a, 57-69
W. Schleiermacher, "Studien an Göttertypen der römischen Rheinprovinzen," *BRGK* 23 (1933) 109-139
K. Schumacher, *Siedlungs- und Kulturgeschichte der Rheinlande* 2 (Mainz 1923) 298-310
F. Stähelin, *op. cit.* in ch. 3
M. J. Vermaseren, *Corpus Inscriptionum et Monumentorum Religionis Mithraicae* 2 (The Hague 1960)
J. de Vries, *La réligion des Celtes* (Paris 1963)
———, *Mithras, the Secret God* (London 1963)

## 7: *Arts and Crafts beyond the Alps*

F. von Bassermann-Jordan, *Der Weinbau der Pfalz im Altertum*[2] (Speyer 1947)
H. Blümner, *Technologie und Terminologie der Gewerbe und Künste bei Griechen und Römer*, vols. 2-4 (Leipzig 1879-87)
O. Brogan, *op. cit.* in ch. 1
F. Brommer, *Zum Mainzer Augustuskopf* (Mainz 1964)
A. W. Byvanck, *Nederland in den Romeinschen Tyd* 2 (Leyden 1944)
J. Como, "Das Grab eines römischen Artzes in Bingen," *G* 9 (1925) 152-162
O. Doppelfeld, *Römisches und Frankisches Glas in Köln* (Köln 1966)
———, 1967a

# Books and Articles Consulted

P. La Baume, *Römisches Kunstgewerbe* (Braunschweig 1964)

S. Loeschke, *Denkmäler vom Weinbau aus der Zeit der Römerherrschaft* (Trier 1923)

W. Ludovici, *Stempelnamen römischer Töpfer von meinen Ausgrabungen in Rheinzabern*, 5 vols. (Munich 1905-1927)

K. Parlasca, *op. cit.* in ch. 2

Pörtner[2]

E. Simon, "Das neugefundene Bildnis des Gaius Caesar in Mainz," *Mainzer Zeitschrift* 58 (1963) 1ff.

F. Sprater, *Die Pfalz unter den Römern* (Speyer 1929/30)

J. A. Stanfield, Grace Simpson, *Central Gaulish Potters* (London 1958)

F. Stähelin, *op. cit.* in ch. 3

J. Szilágyi, *Aquincum* (Budapest 1956)

R. von Uslar, W. Schleiermacher, H. Schoppa, H. von Petrikovits, E. Diez, "Germania Romana 2; Kunst und Kunstgewerbe in römischen Deutschland," *Gymn. Beih.* 5 (1965)

## 8: Afterglow

H. Cüppers, "Vorromische und römische Brücken über die Mosel," *G* 45 (1967) 60-69

F. Drexel, "Die Bilder der Igeler Säule," *Römische Mitteilungen* 38 (1920) 83-142

——, *loc. cit.* in ch. 5.

H. Dragendorff, E. Krüger, *Das Grabmal von Igel* (Trier 1924)

H. Eiden, "Ausgrabungen im spätantiken Trier," *NAD* 340-367

E. Gose, *Das Amphitheater zu Trier*[2] (Trier 1954)

P.E. Hübinger, ed., *Kulturbruch oder Kulturcontinuität im Übergang von der Antike zum Mittelalter* (Darmstadt 1968). A collection of essays by A. Dopsch, H. Aubin, B. Schweizer, K. Böhner, and others.

J.B. Keune, "Colonia Treverorum," *Festschrift Schumacher* (Mainz 1930)

D. Krencker, E. Krüger, *Die Trierer Kaiserthermen* (Augsburg 1929)

W. von Massow, *Das römische Trier* (Berlin 1944)

—— *Die Grabmäler von Neumagen*, 2 vols. (Berlin 1932)

Pörtner[2]

W. Reusch, "Die kaiserliche Palastaula," *Festschrift zur Wiederherstellung der Basilica in Trier* (Trier 1956)

————, *Augusta Treverorum: Rundgang durch das römische Trier*[7] (Trier 1968)

————. "Die Ausgrabungen im Westteil der Trierer Kaiserthermen," G 42 (1964) 92ff.

J. Steinhauser, *Archäologische Siedlungskunde des Trierer Landes* (Trier 1936)

# INDEX

# Index

# Index

Diomedes, 45
Dionysus, 55, 141, 233, 241
*Divitia*, see Deutz
*Divodurum*, see Metz
Doliche, 175
Dolichenus, 175, 176
Domitian (Emp. 81–96), 11, 40, 73, 90, 104, 110, 121, 126, 138
Domitius Ahenobarbus, L., 195
Donar, 159, 162
Doorn, 200
Dorotheenhof, 8
Drusus, Nero Claudius, 59, 61, 62, 64, 69, 70, 84, 87, 88, 90, 91

eau de Cologne, 54
Echzell, 108
Edward VII, 132, 133
Egypt(ian), 176, 177n., 184, 204, 205, 247
Eifel massif, 143, 153, 170, 246
Eining (Abusina), 100, 116
Elbe R., 12, 59, 81, 195
elements, the four, 180
Emperors, deification of, 154
Ems R., 79, 195
Ennius, Q., 234
Enns, 125
Epona, 73, 153, 164, 247
Erato, 233
Erbach-Erbach, Count Franz von, 110
Establishment, British, 154
Establishment, Roman, 159, 195
Esthonians, 13
Etruria, Etruscans, 19, 20, 58
Eugénie, Empress, 132
Eulbach, 110

Feddersen-Wierde, 9, 23
*fibulae*, 9, 10, 20, 82, 95
Finns, 13
Finthen, 162
*Flavia Solva*, 95

Flavian(s), 98, 119, 127, 185
Fochteloo, 10
Fortuna, 40, 109, 143
Frankfurt-am-Main, 125–126, 176, 178
Franks, 53, 69, 90, 225
Frederick the Great, 103
Freya, 161
Friedrich Wilhelm, K. of Prussia, 225
Fuggers, 58
*furor Teutonicus*, 4

Gaeta, 31
Gaius, grandson of Augustus, 187, 195
Galba, Ser. Sulpius (Emp. 68), 135
Gallo-Roman temples, 40, 42, 170, 183
Ganymede, 139, 239
Gaul(s), 3, 12, 30, 31, 33, 51, 54
Gela, 18
Geneva, Lake, 31
Genius
    of the Emperor, 73
    of the Roman People, 156, 239
*Germania Inferior*, see Lower Germany
*Germania Superior*, see Upper Germany
Germanicus Julius Caesar, 79, 84
Gizeh, pyramid of, 185
gladiator mosaic, 212
glassmaking, 207–210
Goethe, J. W. von, 113, 239
Golden Section, 147
Goloring, 27
Good Shepherd, 182
Goths, 13
Grannus, cult title of Apollo, 133
Gratian (Emp. 375–383), 138, 144, 227
Great Pyramid, 185
Great St. Bernard, pass, 54

# Index

# Index

# Index